KAROO FOSSILS
South Africa's first land animals

M.A. Cluver

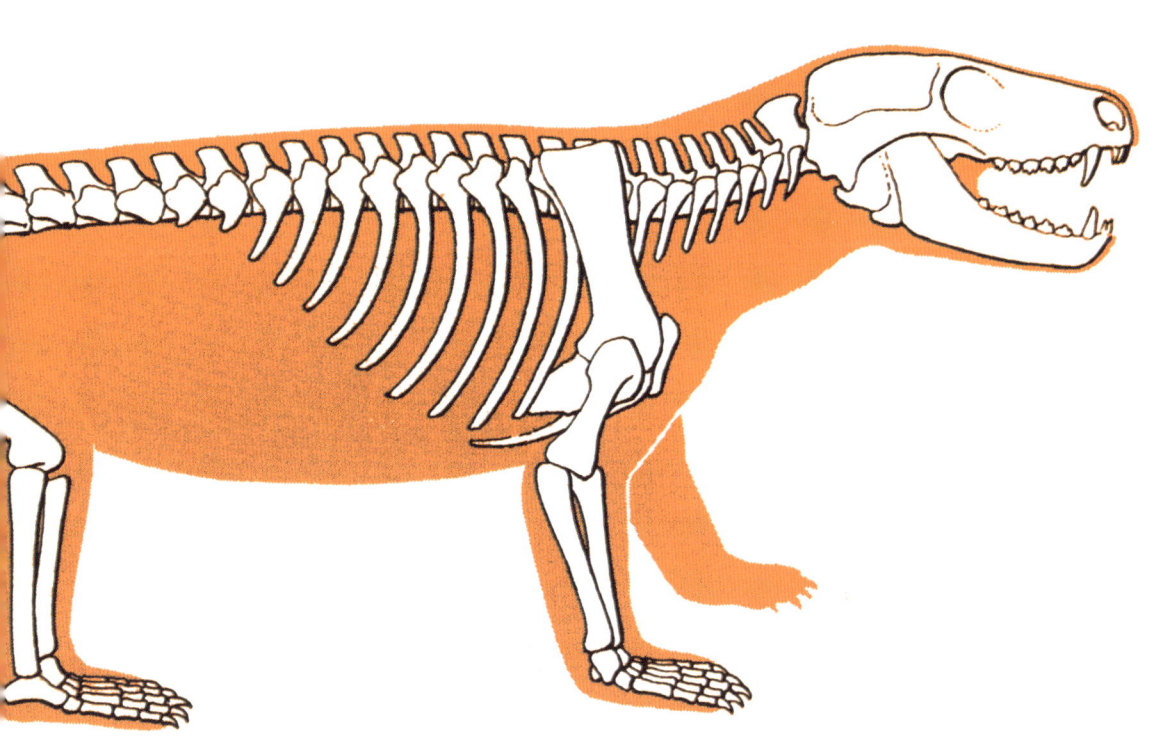

Protea Book House
PRETORIA
2020

Karoo fossils: South Africa's
first land animals – M.A. Cluver

First edition, first impression in 2020 by Protea Book House

PO Box 35110, Menlopark, 0102
1067 Burnett Street, Hatfield, Pretoria
8 Minni Street, Clydesdale, Pretoria
info@proteaboekhuis.co.za
www.proteaboekhuis.com

EDITOR: Danél Hanekom
PROOFREADER: Carmen Hansen-Kruger
COVER AND BOOK DESIGN: Hanli Deysel
FRONT COVER IMAGE: Cedric Hunter
SET IN: 12 on 17 pt ZapfCalligraphy
PRINTED AND BOUND BY TOPPAN LEEFUNG PTE. LTD., CHINA

ILLUSTRATIONS: Cedric Hunter
GRAPHICS: Marietjie du Toit
PHOTOGRAPHS: Roger Smith

ISBN: 978-1-4853-0984-0

Original text © 2020 M.A. Cluver
Published edition © 2020 Protea Book House

No part of this book may be reproduced or transmitted in any form or by any electronic or mechanical means, including photocopying and recording or by any other information storage or retrieval system, without written permission from the publisher.

CONTENTS

007 Introduction

009 The Karoo
013 What the world looked like 300 million years ago
018 The setting of the ancient Karoo
020 The first Karoo animals and their origins
032 Life and death in the ancient Karoo
035 How do we know how old the fossils of the Karoo are?
039 Therapsids and the first mammals
043 The early therapsids
049 The end of the Permian period – when the earth nearly died
059 The later therapsids
066 The archosaurs – a new wave of reptiles
076 The Karoo fossil animals and the ancient supercontinent Gondwana
080 The destiny of the early dinosaurs and mammals of the Karoo
088 Collecting and preserving Karoo fossils
094 Where to see fossils in southern Africa

097 Suggested further reading
099 Glossary
102 Acknowledgements

INTRODUCTION

In 1978 I wrote a book, *Fossil Reptiles of the South African Karoo*, which was published by the then South African Museum (now an important component of Iziko Museums of South Africa), and quickly sold out. This was followed by several reprints. An updated version was published in 1991 and was soon out of print as well. I was pleased to learn that many of the books were bought by people who were living in or were interested in the vast inland semidesert region of South Africa known as the Karoo.

However, since the information in these earlier books was based on scientific evidence of the day, and since scientific research continues to yield more and new information, the 1978 and 1991 versions are now both long outdated. This new book covers more about the Karoo's place on an earlier, very different planet Earth, as well as the extinction events that occurred during the long period that the ancient Karoo animals were the inhabitants of what is now a large part of present-day South Africa.

The fossil record of the Karoo is the only one of its kind and is the source of continuing exploration and research. It is something that South African scientists are proud of and should be treasured as a unique legacy of our prehistory. It is my hope that this book will help generate increased awareness of this aspect of our distant past.

The Karoo

To most people who live in or travel through South Africa, the word "Karoo" conjures up visions of hot, dry plains, bare and flat-topped hills (the "Karoo koppies") and, very often, a long and monotonous highway to be travelled over as quickly as possible. But if you stop along the way and walk out into the wide open spaces surrounding you, you will find that the Karoo holds a fascination of its own – a sense of timelessness, a place of ever-changing colour and character, of unusual animal and plant life and, if you get away from the highways, the experience of an almost complete silence, sometimes broken only by an occasional gust of wind moving across the plains.

At night, well away from the glow of city lights, the Karoo sky is a dark background for a dazzling display of stars which appear to be close enough to reach out to and touch. Small wonder then that the Karoo town of Sutherland was chosen many years ago as a site for an observatory, with the new South African Large Telescope (SALT) now added as one of the world's great optical telescopes. Astronomers use their telescopes to look into deep space; the more distant the stars and galaxies they detect, the longer the time it has taken for their light to reach us here on our planet. Distances are measured in light years, and these scientists are, in fact, looking far back into time as they search for clues to the origin of these stars and galaxies and our place in the universe.

But imagine a very different Karoo to the one we stand in or travel across. Just as astronomers use their telescopes to look back into time, we can also look back millions of years by studying the rocks of the Karoo and discovering a prehistoric world which can be reconstructed and understood only by piecing together a host of sometimes tantalisingly incomplete shreds of evidence. This ancient Karoo of swampy marshlands and wind-blown deserts, populated by a succession of strange, long-extinct animals and plants, is a period of time frozen into the rocks of South Africa and preserved as a treasure trove of knowledge of past life on earth – a vast, barely hidden window into the distant past which is explored by geologists and palaeontologists from around the world. But more: The rock formations that we see as part of today's Karoo landscape stretch much further than what we expect; the Karoo-age geological

formations spread northwards towards the Drakensberg Mountains and eastwards to the coastline of the eastern Cape.

This book is an introduction to the study of the fossils of the South African Karoo, with the intention of drawing attention to this chapter of the prehistoric past, as well as to place in perspective the fascinating creatures which lived during those times and their importance in understanding our own familiar world of today. But to do this properly, we should also understand something of the earth itself as it was at the time.

The Nuweveld Mountains as seen from the Karoo National Park, just south of Beaufort West. Layers of soft shale are capped by thin layers of harder sandstone – oldest layers below, more recent ones above. Fossils are abundant in these rocks. The uppermost layer, forming the crest of the range, is a sheet of hardened volcanic lava of Jurassic age, much younger than the Permian sediments below.

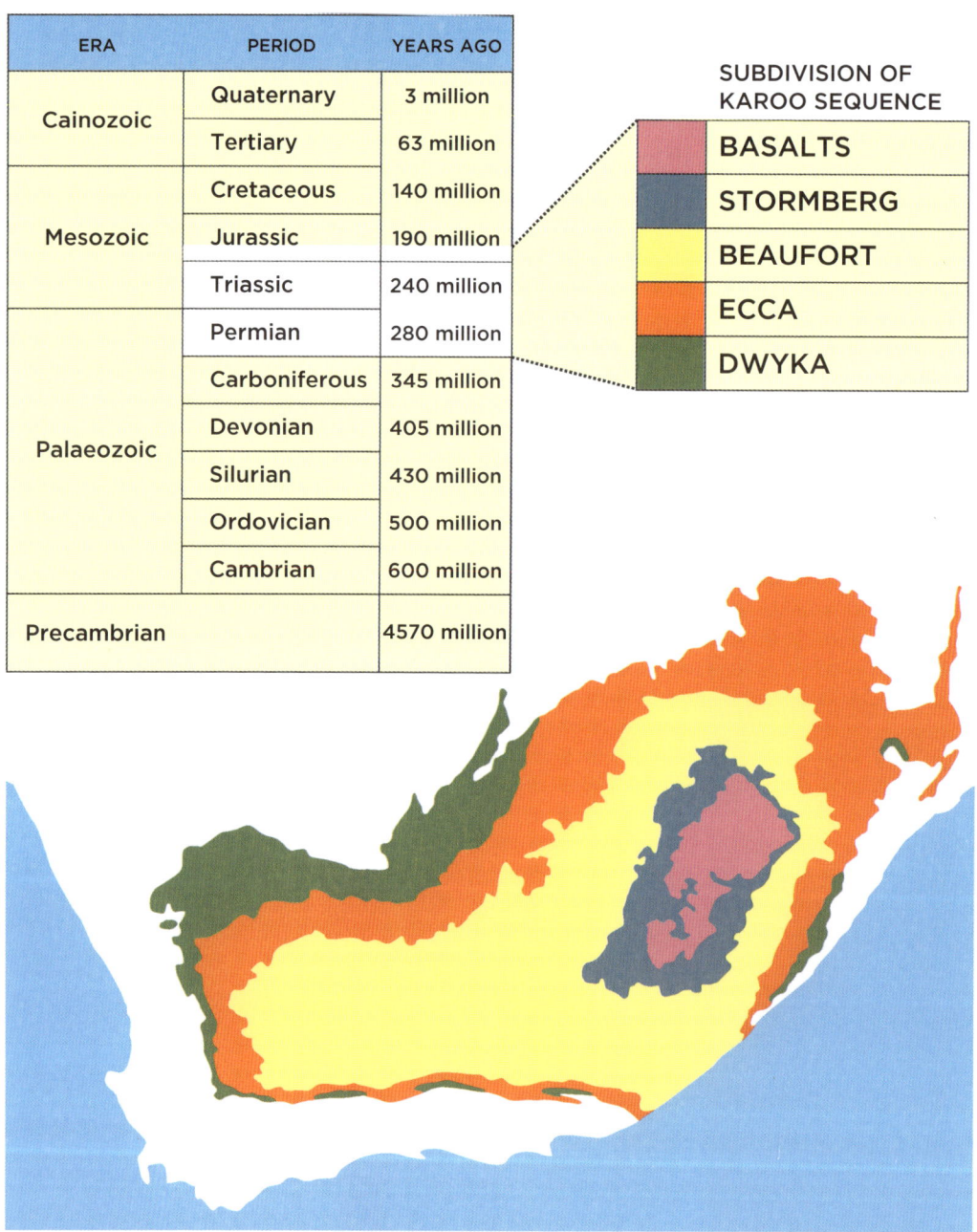

Map showing the areas in South Africa covered by rocks of the Karoo sequence. The oldest Karoo fossils, dating back to around 280 million years ago, are found around Sutherland, Laingsburg and Prince Albert in the southwest, while the youngest fossils, dating back to around 190 million years, occur in the foothills of the Drakensberg Mountains. Karoo fossils are abundant in the areas shown in yellow (Beaufort group) and blue (Stormberg group).

What the world looked like 300 million years ago

To understand the importance of the Karoo fossil record, it is necessary to realise how different the world was at the time when these long-extinct animals and plants lived. Around fifty years ago geologists were gathering evidence that suggested that the continents with which we are familiar today are not the permanent fixtures we always thought they were. As a result of their findings, we now know that continents have **drifted** in the past, and still do so today – but so slowly as to be unnoticed, except by very sensitive measuring instruments.

Continents are the landmasses we live on and see illustrated on maps or in an atlas, and are surrounded by oceans. In fact, they are parts of numerous sections of the earth's outer crust which are known as "plates" – movements of these plates relative to one another are referred to as plate tectonics. For example, the African continent is a part of the earth's crust called the **African plate**; the African plate extends beyond the continent and below sea level and meets other plates deep in the ocean. Areas where plates meet are extremely interesting – our African plate meets the South American plate deep in the Atlantic Ocean, but the plates are actually being forced apart from one another by forces from deep within the earth – hot magma pushing upwards has given rise to undersea mountain ranges in the southern Atlantic.

Recognition of the fact that present-day continents and landmasses once lay in close association with each other, and were then later separated by the process of **plate tectonics** or **continental drift**, is one of the most important developments in recent geological research and helps us understand a great deal more about our planet. Earth is not a static planet where all geological processes have come to an end.

Earthquakes, large or small, which occur from time to time in many places on earth, point to the fact that the interior of our planet is far from stable but is frequently forced to eject molten lava and gases from a deep, super-hot interior. In a few areas, the crust of the earth is weakened along deep cracks – huge geological fault lines – that lie in the ocean beds. These weak zones are characterised by rows of volcanic islands – many with active volcanoes – and "sea mounts", these being submerged ridges formed from lava flowing from the earth's interior through the weakened crust. From these weakened lines in the earth's crust, magma from deep within the earth is forced upward and sideways, pushing the seafloor aside.

The main consequence is that with the seafloor spreading away from such a rift in the earth's crust, **landmasses** are forced to move further apart from one another. But when landmasses – "continental plates" – resist such forces, the spreading seafloor is sometimes forced beneath the resisting landmass – a process known as subduction.

A good example of this is seen today in the North and South American continents. In the Atlantic Ocean, seafloor spreading from mid-Atlantic ridge is slowly pushing these two vast continents to the west. However, in the Pacific, seafloor spreading is trying to force the North and South American continents to the east. The result is that the Pacific Ocean floor is slowly moving beneath the west coasts of North and South America. The coastlines of the western seaboards of these continents are above major subduction zones, and a consequence of the enormous pressures on these two continents is the formation of impressive coastal mountain ranges – the Andes Mountains in South America being a spectacular example.

Naturally, the huge geological pressures involved have consequences: When movements between the sinking seafloor and the mountainous mainland become sudden and abrupt, hugely

WHAT THE WORLD LOOKED LIKE

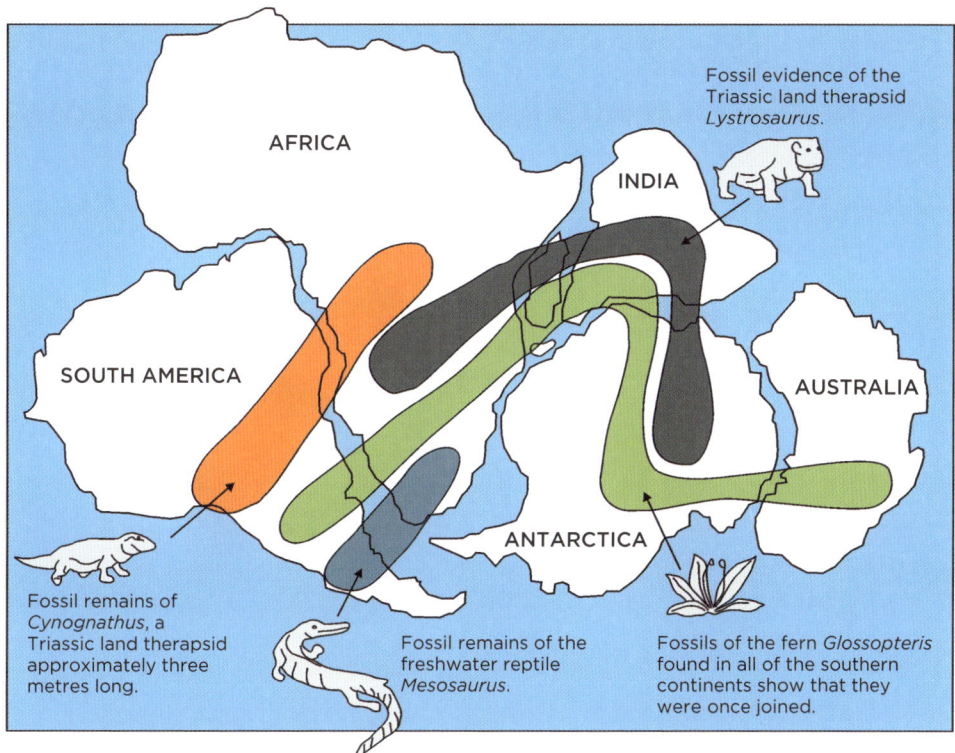

The southern continents as they were joined together during the time that the Karoo was home to early land animals. The chart shows how fossils of these animals, as well as plants, have also been found in South America, India, Australia and Antarctica.

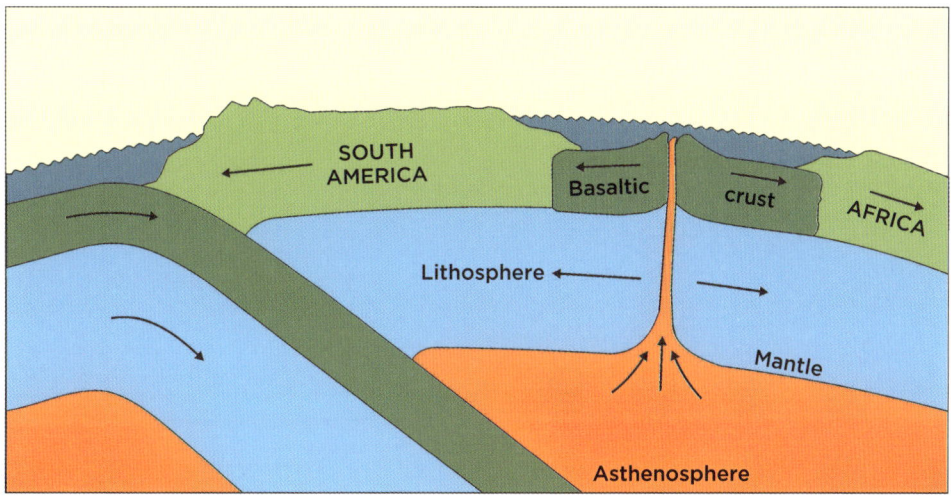

The process of continental drift: highly heated magma arising from deep within the earth forces apart two continental plates, shown here as Africa and South America.

destructive **earthquakes** may occur. For example, on the North American west coast the San Andreas Fault clearly marks the boundary between two gigantic plates. This geological fault line is constantly monitored in an effort to detect signs of a pending major shift in the continental plates so that earthquake warnings can be sent to nearby towns and cities.

But the ancient world was not always like this. At the time that our primitive Karoo animals were alive, all the earth's landmasses, including what is now southern Africa, were locked together into a single giant supercontinent, **Pangaea**. Pangaea was surrounded by a vast ocean but would much later break apart to form what we today recognise as separate continents or subcontinents such as North and South America, Africa, Madagascar, Eurasia, India, Australia and Antarctica. But even before this break-up happened, the original Pangaea was shaped in such a way that a southern section, named **Gondwana**, could clearly be distinguished from a northern one known as Laurasia.

WHAT THE WORLD LOOKED LIKE

GEOLOGICAL TIMETABLE

ERA	PERIOD	BEGAN MILLIONS OF YEARS AGO	SUBDIVISIONS OF KAROO PERIOD
CAINOZOIC	Quarternary	2,6 million years	
	Tertiary	64 million years	
MESOZOIC	Cretaceous	145 million years	
			Drakensberg Basalts: 182 million years ago
	Jurassic	201 million years	
			Stormberg
	Triassic	250 million years	
			Beaufort
PALAEOZOIC	Permian	298 million years	Beaufort
			Ecca
	Carboniferous	358 million years	
	Devonian	419 million years	
	Silurian	443 million years	
	Ordovician	485 million years	
	Cambrian	541 million years	
PRECAMBRIAN	The earliest geological period. The Precambrian rock formations date from around 4570 to 541 million years.		

The Karoo period is divided into the Ecca (oldest), the Beaufort, the Stormberg and (youngest) the Drakensberg basalts. The latter formed from molten lava forced up from deep within the earth.

The setting of the ancient Karoo

During the early Permian period, around 290 million years ago, **Gondwana** was slowly emerging from the grip of a great Ice Age. Thick sheets of ice, which had for thousands of years covered the surface of the future South Africa, were melting to leave behind a vast inland sea which extended from the present-day Laingsburg and Prince Albert in the south to Kroonstad and Volksrust in the north, and from Calvinia and Kimberley in the west to Pietermaritzburg and East London to the east.

To geologists this ancient low-lying area, surrounded by uplands and mountains, is known as the **Karoo Basin**, and the layers of sediment which filled the basin and became layers of rock are known as the **Karoo Supergroup**. It is within these rocks that the long story of Karoo life unfolded. For more than 80 million years, from the Middle Permian period through the following Triassic period and into the beginning of the Jurassic period, the Karoo Basin supported animal and plant life, and the fossilised remains of these extinct organisms reveal a saga of successes and failures, and the emergence and decline of many varied forms of life.

Some of the creatures which made an appearance in the Karoo Basin survive in modified form today – crocodiles are an example, as are mammals, whose early ancestral forerunners made up a large component of the Karoo reptiles. As we shall see, some other areas of Gondwana and parts of Pangaea were also home to some animals which were closely related to those which flourished in the Karoo of South Africa.

The uniqueness of the Karoo is largely due to the fact that its 90-million-year fossil record, covering a period from 270 to less than

190 million years ago, is almost unbroken, so that intricate evolutionary pathways followed by different animal groups through time can be more accurately traced than in similar fossil-bearing rock formations in other parts of the world.

In the palaeontological sense, therefore, the Karoo is more than just a geographical area; it is a window into a time long past, when a very different landscape was inhabited by animals which have been extinct for millions of years.

The first Karoo animals and their origins

With the retreat of the ice sheets, the climate of the Karoo Basin became more temperate and was characterised by periodic rainfalls and flooding of some areas surrounding the new inland sea. A varied and, in places, lush vegetation arose, and in the northern part of the basin the fossilised remains of these ancient plants formed the rich coal seams which are today still of economic importance and the main source of electricity generated in South Africa. This inland sea was populated by a number of creatures, some of which would be recognisable today as bivalves and insects. One group, which would scare anyone if they were still present today, are the eurypterids – up to two-metre-long "sea scorpions" which fed on small creatures on the bottoms of lakes. Trackways of eurypterids have been found in rocks formed at the basin of these lakes, and a full-sized specimen has been found in rock strata near Prince Albert in today's southern Karoo. In addition, a small aquatic reptile, *Mesosaurus*, the oldest of the Karoo fossil animals, has been found in some abundance, also at a locality in present-day Namibia, in rock sediments which once formed at the bottom of this inland sea. ***Mesosaurus*** is one of the earliest known reptiles which left a life on land to return to an aquatic lifestyle, apparently feeding on small fish and invertebrates. More about this small but remarkable animal later.

But for millions of years the Karoo Basin was, as far as we know, without significant animal life on land. It was not until about 270 million years ago, in the middle **Permian period**, that South Africa's first terrestrial animals appeared – ancient immigrants from other parts of the world.

The emergence of land animals such as these is a story in itself:

THE FIRST KAROO ANIMALS AND THEIR ORIGINS 21

Amphibians, which were present in watery environments such as those of the early Karoo, are confined to a lifestyle which required them to lay their eggs in water. However, fossils from much older localities in the present northern hemisphere clearly show a steady development of the ability of creatures to move towards an increasingly dominant presence on land. The last boundary preventing them from a permanent life on land was the need to lay eggs in water. This barrier was finally overcome by a major evolutionary step: the development of the **amniote egg**. The amniote egg has

Mesosaurus, known from fossils in Dwyka shales. This aquatic reptile, reaching about 40 centimetres in length, lived some time before the land animals of the Karoo appeared in South Africa. Fossils of *Mesosaurus* are also found in similar rocks in South America.

a protective membrane (the amnion) which allowed animals to lay their eggs safely on land. The amnion membrane provided protection from drying in the open air as well as allowing the exchange of air between the developing embryo and the surrounding atmosphere. From these early land animals, known collectively as amniotes, all later land animals evolved.

Today amniotes include reptiles, birds, crocodiles, and mammals; most of the Karoo vertebrate fossils were fully developed amniotes. As we noted above, the little *Mesosaurus* seemed to have been greatly attracted to an abundance of small prey in the surrounding waters, and went back to an aquatic lifestyle, which raises the interesting question of whether it was therefore obliged to return to land to lay its eggs, such as modern crocodiles and sea turtles regularly have to do. In any event, *Mesosaurus* was well adapted to an aquatic life; rows of sharp teeth on their relatively long jaws were ideal for capturing small animals, and their ribs are unusually thick and heavy – very likely to assist them in swimming down to deep water. Small pebbles found in the rib-cage region of some specimens would have reduced the body's buoyancy, adding to the suggestion that *Mesosaurus* was prepared to dive deeply with little effort. As mentioned earlier, *Mesosaurus* is so far the earliest known fossil animal in the Karoo record and is estimated to have lived at close to 280 million years ago – well before the appearance of the later Karoo land animals.

The first Karoo land animals were as varied in size as in kind. Large, lumbering plant-eating types co-existed with small, active predators, and groups of small plant-eaters lived in the shadow of awesome flesh-eating giants. In fact, fossils of these early Karoo animals show that they formed an ecologically balanced fauna,

> Three early Karoo animals. *Struthiocephalus* (top) was a three-metre-long herbivorous dinocephalian, while the similar-sized *Anteosaurus* (centre) was a related carnivorous species. The plant-eating *Bradysaurus* (bottom) was a cotylosaurian reptile retaining primitive characteristics of the first stem-reptiles.

THE FIRST KAROO ANIMALS AND THEIR ORIGINS

with a high percentage of **herbivores** (plant-eaters) and a low percentage of **carnivores** (flesh-eaters). It is also apparent that the animals were adapted to a variety of lifestyles and that they quite likely fully exploited all the available habitats.

The first Karoo vertebrates belonged to two main groups: the so-called **parareptiles** and the **therapsids**. The most common parareptiles were pareiasaurs, related to primitive ancestral reptiles which are known from fossil localities in today's northern hemisphere. The pareiasaurs were bulky herbivores, reaching an average body length of over 2,5 metres, and were an important group in the early Karoo. The fossilised skeletons of these animals are often found complete and largely undisturbed, and it is likely that many of the pareiasaurs died after becoming trapped in soft, yielding mud in which their bodies were preserved beyond the reach of scavenging carnivores.

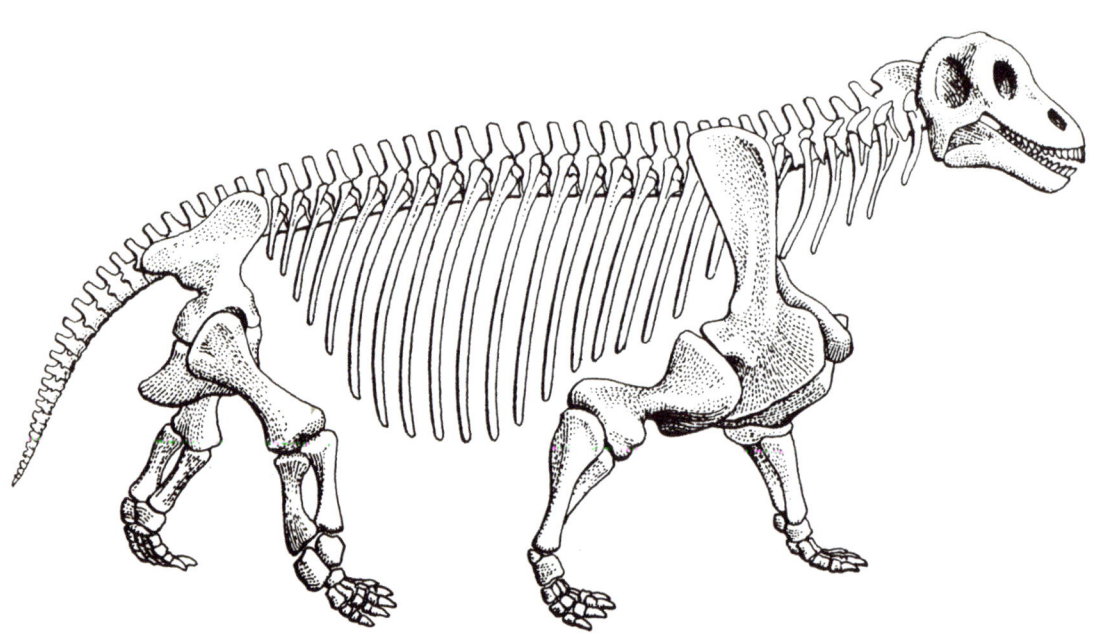

Skeleton of the dinocephalian *Moschops* about 2,5 metres long. The bones of the skull have undergone enormous thickening.

The second group, up until recently referred to as mammal-like reptiles, are now known to have evolved from a group separate from the ancestors of true reptiles and are classified as Therapsida. The Therapsida were the dominant animals of the early Karoo and were representatives of a particularly important branch of evolution. The Therapsida were named "mammal-like reptiles" in earlier studies because they display a number of features in their preserved skeletons which set them apart from other reptiles, and which resemble those seen in the first true mammals – which appeared as small creatures many millions of years later.

The therapsids were from the start a highly diversified assemblage of animals. Most impressive were the **Dinocephalia**, almost universally large and strongly built animals that included flesh-

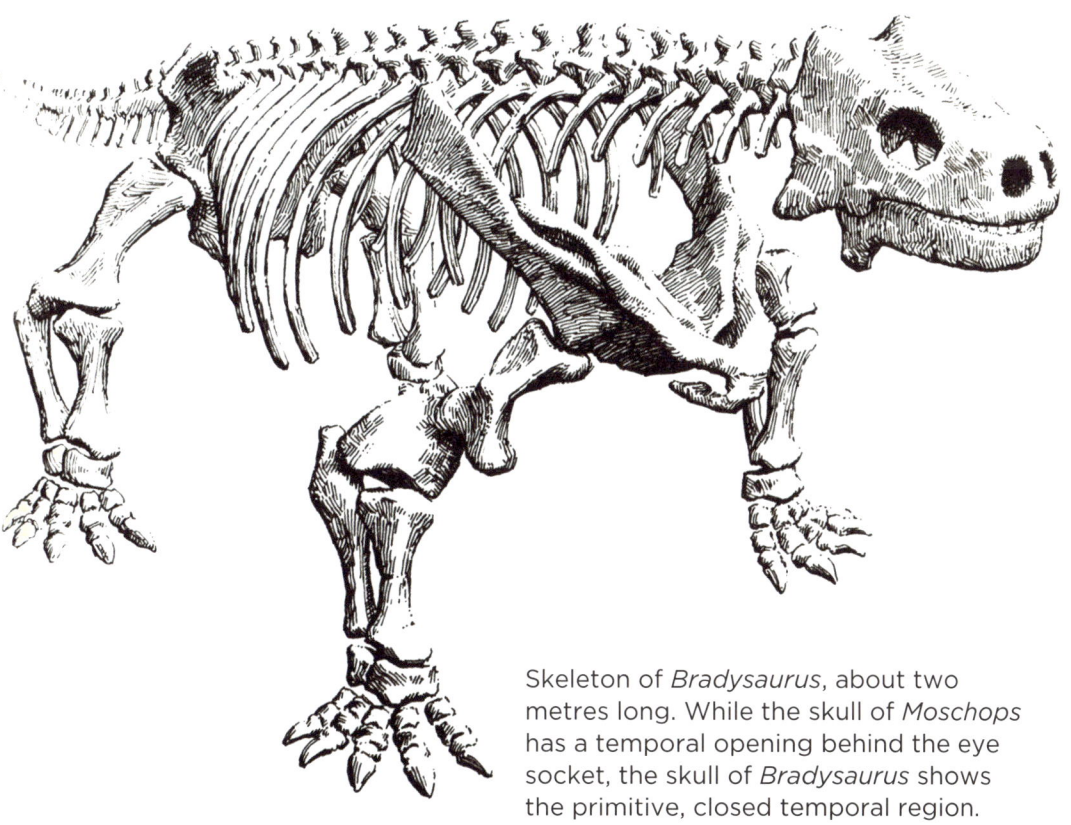

Skeleton of *Bradysaurus*, about two metres long. While the skull of *Moschops* has a temporal opening behind the eye socket, the skull of *Bradysaurus* shows the primitive, closed temporal region.

eaters, such as *Anteosaurus*, and lumbering herbivores such as *Tapinocephalus* and *Moschops*. The herbivorous dinocephalians are characterised by thickening of most bones of the skull, and while some palaeontologists suggest that such thickening was of little adaptive significance, another theory maintains that the thick and strong skull bones indicate that at least some of these herbivorous dinocephalians were adapted for head-butting – as is seen in some living mammals, especially in instances where territory is contested.

Alongside the dinocephalians were other carnivorous flesh-eating animals, the gorgonopsians and therocephalians. Gorgonopsians were not common in the early Karoo record but flourished in later times. **Therocephalians** were more progressive in their development and included a number of different families even at this early stage of the Karoo's history, with *Scymnosaurus* and *Pristerognathus* as powerful and formidable predators. Also present were members of a group known as the Biarmosuchia. Recent research has shown that these were in fact the most primitive of the therapsids. Karoo biarmosuchians include *Burnetia* and *Hipposaurus* – the latter previously classified as a gorgonopsian.

The **Dicynodontia**, which together with the pareiasaurians and some dinocephalians rank among the earliest well-adapted herbivores, were initially small animals. Very common throughout most of the Karoo period, these unusual animals had a highly modified skull structure, with most or all teeth replaced by a horn-covered beak or bill – much like that seen in today's tortoises and turtles. Evidence from fossil trackway sites show that it is very probable that at least some dicynodonts lived in small groups or herds.

These were by no means the only animals living in the early Karoo. As mentioned earlier, several primitive amphibians and freshwater fishes are known, together with a variety of invertebrates. A most interesting early member of the Karoo animals was the little *Eunotosaurus*, distinguished by its flattened, wide ribs and now recognised as the most ancient member of modern-day turtles. The

Two carnivorous therapsids encounter beaked dicynodonts. *Scymnosaurus* (top) was a 2,5-metre-long therocephalian, while *Hipposaurus* (bottom) was a 1,2-metre-long gorgonopsian. Both flesh-eaters are known from the earliest fossil-bearing rocks of the Beaufort group.

landscape was, however, dominated by the reptilian pareiasaurs and the therapsids, and the question arises – where did these animals come from?

Comparisons with fossils from other parts of the world have indicated an eastern European origin of the early Karoo fauna. Very similar primitive therapsids are known from rock formations in Russia and China, and recent discoveries in the southern Karoo have greatly strengthened the relationships between early Russian

The pelycosaur *Dimetrodon*, a member of the group of reptiles ancestral to the therapsids of the Karoo. *Dimetrodon*, about 3,5 metres long, carried an unusual sail-like crest on its back, supported by bony extensions of the vertebrae.

and South African fossils. The ancestry of the primitive Russian therapsids can in turn be traced back to members of an even earlier reptile group, the pelycosaurs, which are best known from fossils in North America. Taking into account the fact that continents which are now separated were then parts of the single landmass of Pangaea, it seems that South Africa's first land animals were relatives of groups which were then present in parts of Pangaea, but that passages existed which allowed migration between the southern and northern part of Pangaea. However, while the northern hemisphere record of animals related to those found in the Karoo is patchy (but vitally

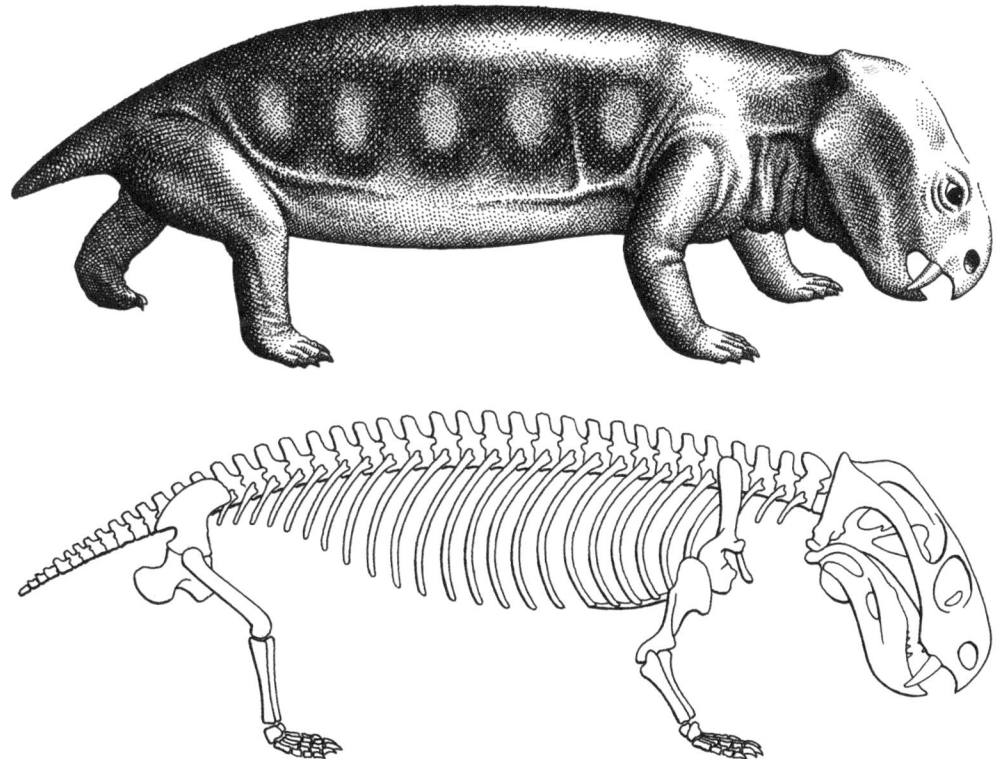

The dicynodont *Emydops*. Dicynodonts were herbivorous therapsids common throughout nearly the entire Karoo period, and ranged in body length from less than 20 centimetres to over two metres. In the skull the lower jaw became very mobile and teeth were partly or altogether replaced by horny beaks.

important), present-day southern Africa appears to have by far the best record of especially the Permian and Triassic terrestrial fauna.

Conditions in the Karoo Basin in South Africa seem to have been especially well suited for providing a record of the continued evolution and development of this fauna. But many of the well-known Karoo Permian- and Triassic-age fossils have also been found in localities in Namibia, Zimbabwe, Zambia and even Madagascar, and are evidence of a widespread vertebrate fauna linked to the abundant Karoo fossils. So it is important to note that, although the Karoo fossil record is a literal treasure trove of Permian and Triassic vertebrate fossils, many similar animals were living in other parts of the world. And, as will be seen later, the early Karoo-age animals were followed by several waves of "immigration" by other terrestrial creatures, to make up the full Karoo fossil record.

The Karoo's long and largely unbroken history of land life over a period of millions of years reveals ever-changing patterns as some groups disappear and new ones appear. We shall see later that several animal groups became extinct fairly suddenly, while a major **extinction event** at the end of the Permian period – one of the largest ever recorded – resulted in a huge reduction in the Karoo fauna, leaving only a few survivors at the beginning of the following Triassic period.

The formidable gorgonopsian *Rubidgea*, with a body length of over two metres, stalks the dicynodont *Diictodon*. *Rubidgea* was among the last of the Karoo gorgonopsians, a group which did not survive beyond the end of the Permian period.

Life and death in the ancient Karoo

The struggle for survival was as much a feature of life in the ancient Karoo as it is a feature of animal life today. Competition for food and territory and evading predators were all-important matters in the day-to-day life of these animals. Death – and eventually extinction – was the ultimate fate of those species that were ill-equipped for the struggle. Ironically, it is through death and a fortunate process of fossilisation that we can today obtain glimpses of life in such bygone environments as the Karoo of more than 200 million years ago.

The chances of an animal skeleton being preserved as a fossil are in fact very small. **Fossilisation** is possible only if the animal's carcass is made inaccessible to predators and scavengers almost immediately after death, for instance, through rapid burial in soft sand or mud, or removal by flowing water to eventually come to rest in mud or clay at the bottom of a pool or lake. In the absence of extensive microbial activity, the hard parts of the body, such as the bones and teeth, are preserved by gradual replacement of their original chemical composition by minerals from the surrounding mud or clay sediments. Depending on the conditions of the burial, the pro-

A: The carcass of a Karoo animal is washed into a small lake, where it sinks to the bottom and decomposes. After some time has passed, only the bones and teeth remain. **B:** Fine mud and clay settling on the bottom of the lake cover the decomposing body. Chemical substances from the mud penetrate the bones, preserving them from decay. With the passage of time, the mud and clay gradually harden into rock, and the now fossilised skeleton may remain unchanged for many millions of years. **C:** Erosion has exposed the rock strata that formed at the bottom of the ancient Karoo lake, and parts of the fossilised skeleton can be seen. Careful excavation will be required to remove the skeleton from the surrounding rock.

cess of replacement may take place over many years – even millennia – or may be completed within a fairly short space of time. Once a skeleton is entombed and mineralised in this way, it is preserved for as long as the surrounding rock, which is itself formed by hardening of the original sediments, remains undisturbed.

Only when **erosion** of the enclosing rock layers takes place do the fossilised remains become exposed. Erosion of the Karoo rock formations commenced around 110 million years ago after the originally low-lying central area of South Africa was uplifted by forces deep within the earth's crust, as the supercontinent Pangaea began to break apart into the continents we have today. For the first time, rivers started flowing from the uppermost Karoo rocks to the new seas surrounding South Africa, gradually eroding and exposing sediments formed millions of years earlier.

Although the Karoo rocks provide us with a wonderful fossil record that tells us a great deal about animal life at the time, it should be remembered that the conditions that allow fossils to form and remain preserved are best found in sedimentary rocks formed from pools or swamps or the banks of ancient river systems. Creatures adapted for life in upland areas are much less likely to be found as fossils, since their remains would be more likely to have been exposed long enough to disintegrate or be devoured by scavengers. The fact that some species found in Karoo rocks are known from very few, or even single specimens, indicates that the fossil record that we rely on is very likely far from the full picture of life during the Permian and Triassic periods.

How do we know how old the fossils of the Karoo are?

We know that the Karoo rocks that we see today cover a very long period of geological time, and that the earliest fossil reptiles found in the oldest rock layers were followed by other, more advanced forms in later times. But how do we know which the oldest or youngest layers are, and how do we know how old these rocks actually are?

Based on fossils found today, the Karoo rocks can be divided into a vertical succession of several so-called **assemblage zones**, totalling a thickness of many thousands of metres. Each zone, representing a time span of millions of years, is characterised by a fossil species which is only found in that time interval. The earliest zone, the *Eodicynodon* assemblage zone, is named after a primitive herbivorous therapsid – referred to again later – which is only found in strata of this part of the Karoo succession. In addition, the Karoo zones are often characterised by different **sedimentary** rock types, which reflect to a large extent the prevailing climate of the period.

Therefore, widespread and thick layers of coarse sandstone indicate extensive flooding, whereby large amounts of sand and silt were carried down into the Karoo swamps by rapidly flowing water. Slow-moving streams, on the other hand, carried fine mud or clay into the basin and these sediments, hardened into layers of shale, are indications of milder periods. Similarly, dry, desert-like conditions may result in rock layers consisting of rounded, wind-blown sand grains. Within the extremes such as these are many intermediate rock types reflecting the climate changes that occurred during the Karoo period.

HOW DO WE KNOW HOW OLD FOSSILS ARE?

The order of succession of the Karoo zones conforms to the geological principle that older sedimentary rock layers lie below the succeeding younger ones. The rocks of the early *Eodicynodon* assemblage zone, just below the next *Tapinocephalus* assemblage zone, are the lowest and therefore the oldest of the Karoo zones, while the youngest assemblage zone, where early dinosaur remains are found, lies at the very top of the succession. At no one place are all the Karoo assemblage zones exposed together, and the correlation of these zones from various outcrops is an ongoing task in Karoo palaeontology and geology.

But if palaeontologists can speak in terms of millions of years, how do they know how old their fossils are? By dividing the Karoo into a succession of zones, fossils from different levels can be dated relative to each other, since we know that the lower zones must be older than the upper ones. Such relative dating is often all that is required by the palaeontologist, but it is also most important to know the actual age of fossils. One way of determining such **absolute dating** is to measure the radioactive elements that are present in certain rock types. This is made possible, for example, by the fact that fresh lava or basalt contains measurable amounts of radioactive uranium which, as soon as the lava cools and hardens, starts breaking down steadily at a constant rate, like a clock running from 12 noon to 12 midnight, into less complex radioactive matter until it is finally transformed into lead. Samples taken from such basaltic rocks can lead to an indication of how long the "clock" has been running, and therefore how old the rock is. With a so-called **radiometric age** determined, we can then estimate the age of the older sedimentary rocks which lie immediately below a basalt rock layer or volcanic ash bed. Such beds of ancient ash and lava occur in the Karoo and are important in assisting with dating of the sequence of Karoo sedimentary rocks. New dating techniques on Karoo rocks are being used on an ongoing basis, helping to pinpoint actual timeframes when major changes in the fossil fauna, such as extinction events, occurred.

HOW DO WE KNOW HOW OLD FOSSILS ARE?

KAROO SUPERGROUP

GEOLOGICAL AGES IN MILLION YEARS	KAROO GROUP	ASSEMBLAGE ZONE
JURASSIC Jurassic began 199 million years ago	**Drakensberg basalts** **Stormberg:** Clarens formation	
TRIASSIC Triassic began 250 million years ago	**Stormberg:** Elliot formation **Stormberg:** Molteno formation Beaufort Beaufort	 *Cynognathus* zone *Lystrosaurus* zone
UPPER PERMIAN 272 million years ago Permian began 298 million years ago	Beaufort Beaufort Beaufort Beaufort Beaufort Ecca	*Daptocephalus* zone *Cistecephalus* zone *Tropidostoma* zone *Pristerognathus* zone *Eodicynodon* zone *Mesosaurus*

The **assemblage zone** concept is vitally important in studies of the Karoo fossil reptiles. New fossil localities continue to be discovered and explored, and help to refine the boundaries of these zones as well as introduce new ones. By tracing the fossil record through these various time zones, the effects on the animals of a changing environment are seen in the success of some groups and the failure of others. The evolution of this part of life's history is seen as an ever-changing pattern, where an infinite number of organisms each in turn enjoy a momentary appearance before succumbing to the oblivion of a seemingly inevitable extinction.

Therapsids and the first mammals

The most significant of the Karoo animals are undoubtedly the Therapsida. The Karoo Basin provided a setting for the evolution of this group into progressively more and more advanced forms, leading eventually to the rise of the first mammals. To fully appreciate the fundamental nature of the changes involved in this transition from therapsids to mammals, the contrasts between reptiles and mammals must be considered.

The earliest back-boned animals to fully exploit existence on land were cold-blooded, egg-laying animals with bodies which were sometimes scale-covered. The term "**cold-blooded**" means that the animal cannot maintain a constant body temperature; in fact, this is influenced by and fluctuates with that of the environment. Reptiles are sluggish in cold surroundings but become active under warm conditions.

Mammals, on the other hand, are active, **warm-blooded**, fur-covered animals which give birth to live young. Newly born offspring are suckled on milk-like fluids produced by mammary glands of the female, and parental care is usually vital to the rearing of the young. Mammals, with an advanced physiology, maintain a constant body temperature which is largely independent of that of the environment. Fur and sweat glands help in warming or cooling the body, and physiologically therefore mammals are more advanced than reptiles and capable of sustained activity in a variety of environmental conditions. Body scales are almost universally absent.

These differences between reptiles and mammals are reflected in many ways in the bony skeletons of the two groups. Increased locomotory activity in mammals is accompanied by changes in

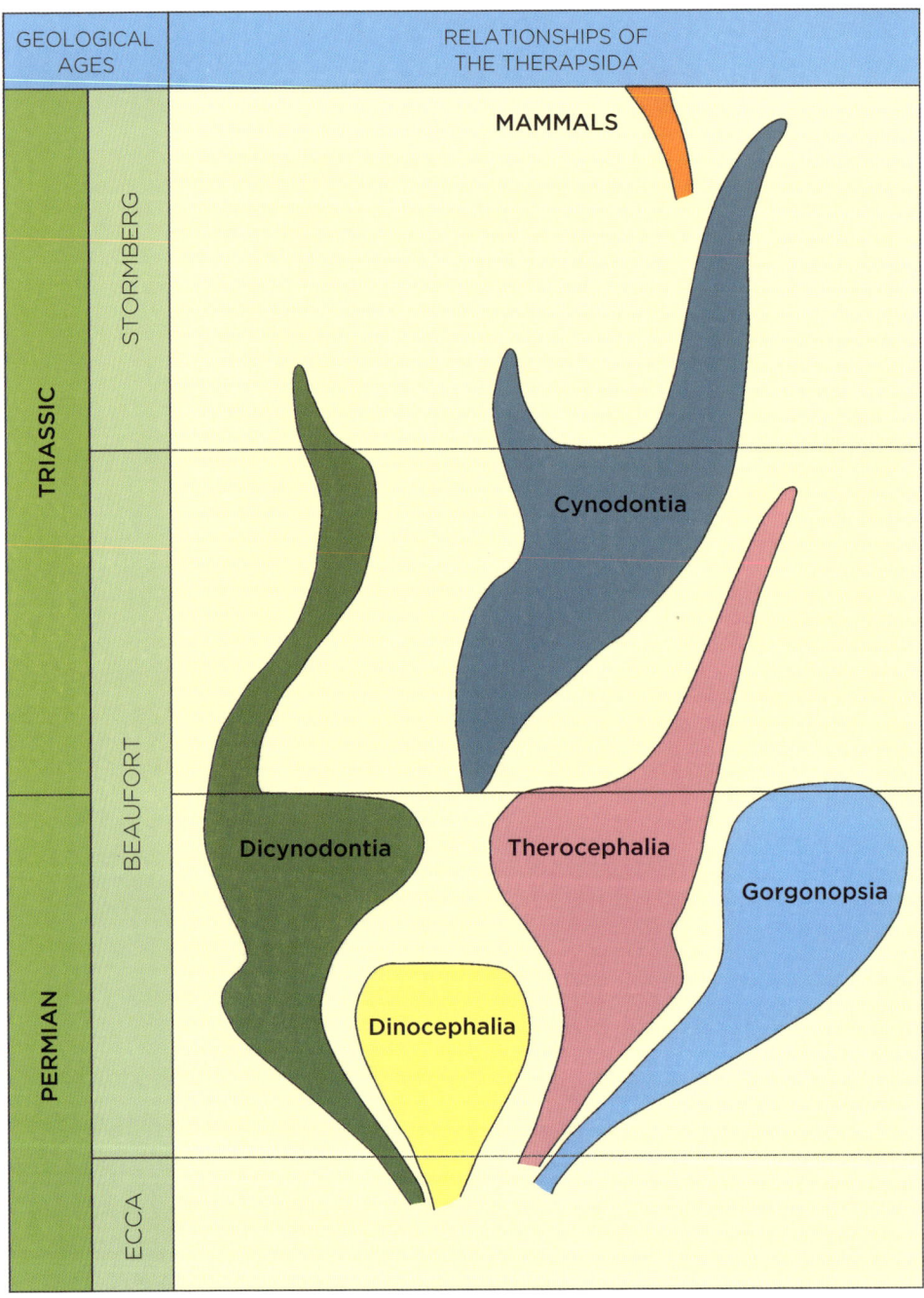

Diagram showing the relationships between the various Therapsida. Therapsida did not survive beyond the end of the Triassic period, but one group, the Cynodontia, gave rise to the first mammals at the end of the Triassic, about 200 million years ago.

THERAPSIDS AND THE FIRST MAMMALS

The dog, a mammal, differs in many respects from the crocodile, a reptile. The dog is warm-blooded, furry and capable of long periods of activity. The crocodile is "cold-blooded" in the sense that it cannot control its body temperature, scaly skinned and capable of only short (but vicious!) bursts of activity.

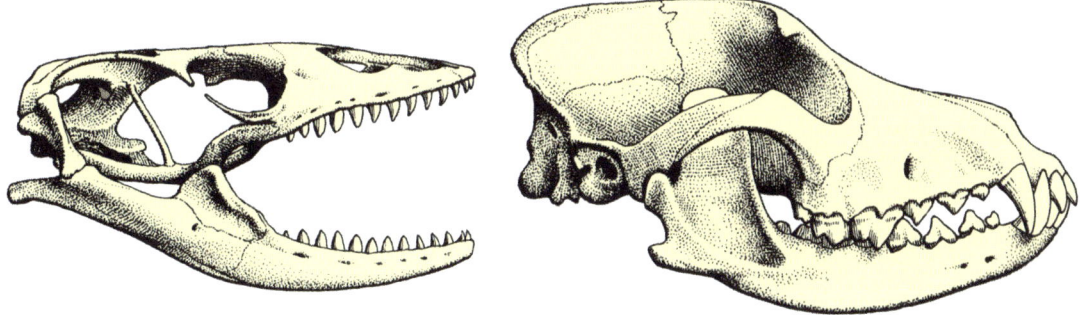

The skull of a reptile (the leguaan *Varanus niloticus*) compared with that of a mammal (the dog *Canis familiaris*). In the reptile there are a number of bones in the lower jaw, and the teeth are all uniform and pointed. The bones of the skull are loosely connected to each other. In the mammal the lower jaw consists of a single bone, and teeth are divided into incisors, canines, premolars and molars – very different from those of the reptile. In mammals, too, the skull bones are firmly attached to each other.

the shape and length of the limb bones, while the relatively large brain of mammals requires a sturdier skull than the reptilian one. Also, to maintain physiological processes, improved feeding and chewing functions are needed and can be seen in the structure and arrangement of the teeth. In addition, the chewing process in mammals requires a firm and rigid lower jaw. In reptiles each half of the lower jaw consists of several separate bones, while in mammals only a single enlarged bone, the dentary, is present.

These are only a few of the skeletal differences which exist between a typical reptile and mammal, and they can be seen in varying degrees of development in fossils of the transitional so-called "mammal-like reptiles" of the Karoo.

The early therapsids

The **Dinocephalia**, mentioned earlier, were among the most primitive of the mammal-like therapsids, but some of their features, particularly of the skull, serve to illustrate the fundamental differences from true reptiles. In contrast to that of most other reptiles, the skull itself is a firmly knit structure with little or no internal flexibility between the constituent bones. A large opening in the temporal region, behind the eye socket, permitted bulging of the jaw muscles during chewing and biting, and is a characteristic of all therapsids. The tooth row, which in reptiles usually consists of a line of simple, undifferentiated teeth, is in most of the Dinocephalia divided into functionally distinct incisors, canines and postcanines, the latter foreshadowing the mammalian premolars and molars. The Dinocephalia, although primitive members of the mammal-like therapsid stock, were therefore altogether distinct from reptile groups, but it is unlikely that mammalian characteristics such as hair, mammary glands and "warm-bloodedness" were present among them. The Dinocephalia, which were mostly large animals, included both carnivorous and herbivorous species. These early animals did not survive beyond the *Tapinocephalus* assemblage zone, and were in effect an early, sterile offshoot of the therapsids of the Karoo.

Another widespread group, the **Dicynodontia**, are well represented in the Karoo fossil record and are the most numerous of the fossils found there. With specialisations like horn-covered beak-like mouthparts and a highly modified method for chewing, these were clearly herbivorous creatures. The huge diversity of dicynodont species so far identified suggests that this unusual but clearly effective feeding system, which sets them apart from other therapsids, made it possible for them to exploit many different environments and vegetation types, and thereby take on an almost global distribution during the late Permian and Triassic periods. They have been identified in East Africa, India, North and South America, Russia, China, Antarctica and Scotland, and more recently in Madagascar. Fragmentary remains indicate that they may also have been present in what is present-day Australia. In **South Africa**, the earliest dicynodont known is *Eodicynodon*, found near the town of Prince Albert in the southern Karoo in rocks at the base of the Beaufort succession. *Eodicynodon* displays several features which make it more primitive than later dicynodonts.

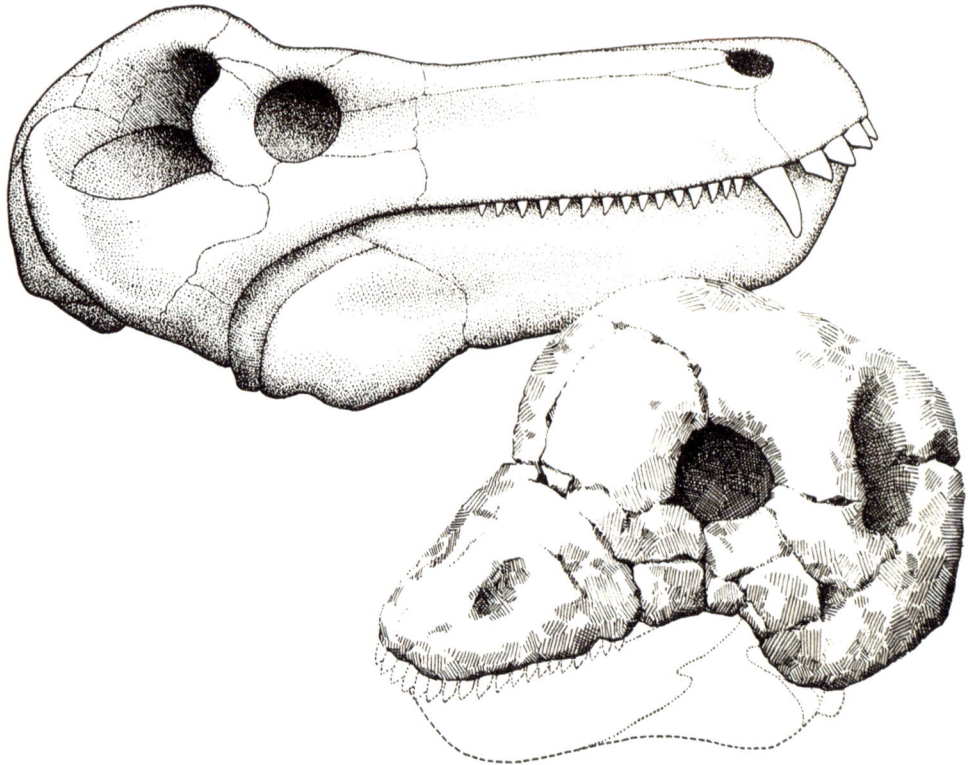

Skulls of two early therapsids, the dinocephalians *Tapinosuchus* (top) and *Tapinocephalus* (below). As in all therapsids, there is a single opening in the skull behind the eye socket. In *Tapinocephalus* the bones of the skull are greatly thickened and firmly fused with each other. The Dinocephalia were generally large animals, with bodies of up to three metres long.

The carnivorous **Gorgonopsia**, after humble beginnings in *Tapinocephalus* assemblage zone times, flourished in succeeding assemblage zones, but did not survive after the end of the Permian period. However, another early therapsid group, the **Therocephalia**, were from the beginning a progressive and flourishing carnivorous group and it is likely that the line leading to the earliest mammals ran through them and their descendants, the cynodonts.

The end of the *Tapinocephalus* assemblage zone is marked by the disappearance of the Dinocephalia, many pareiasaur species and a considerable reduction in the number of Therocephalia. In the following Upper Permian *Pristerognathus* assemblage zone, the Karoo animals were smaller in size. Gone were the large dinocephalians, both herbivores and flesh-eaters, and dicynodonts became more common but remained relatively small. This sudden change in the fossil record suggests at the very least a significant shift in climate and environmental conditions – a mini-extinction event for the animals which could not adapt to new Karoo conditions. The Karoo sequence, covering millions of years, illustrates several such changes from time to time, where previously abundant species suddenly disappear from the fossil record and are replaced by newcomers. However, none of these phenomena were as disastrous as the worldwide end-Permian extinction event – more about this later.

Later **Permian dicynodonts**, such as *Endothiodon* and *Daptocephalus*, are mainly large in size with *Endothiodon* possessing a powerful row of cheek teeth in addition to its horny beak. In *Daptocephalus* on the other hand, teeth other than a pair of large tusks were absent. *Cistecephalus* was a small animal with a box-like skull, and both skull and skeleton strongly suggest that *Cistecephalus* may have burrowed into the soft soil of the Karoo as an important part of their lifestyle.

Besides these, a considerable number of other dicynodonts, large and small in size, were abundant in the marshy Karoo lowlands. *Diictodon*, a smallish animal which has also been found in China, was the most abundant dicynodont in later Permian times, and there

Two nearly complete skeletons of the dicynodont *Diictodon*, discovered together in the Beaufort West district. *Diictodon* was one of the most common therapsids during the early stages of the Karoo sequence, but did not survive after the end-Permian extinction event.

is strong evidence that this species was also an accomplished burrower. Several preserved burrows, containing the fossilised remains of skeletons of *Diictodon*, have been uncovered. *Tropidostoma, Aulacephalodon, Dicynodon,* and *Oudenodon* (the latter recently also discovered in Madagascar) were common dicynodonts in latest Permian times.

Together with the Therapsida, advanced **pareiasaurs** – including some dwarf species – were present in the late Permian fossil record of the Karoo, but in limited numbers only, while gorgonopsians such as *Rubidgea* were relatively plentiful. The latter were large and powerful carnivores with greatly enlarged incisors and canines but with few or no postcanine teeth. Chewing or crushing of food had not yet developed in these animals and flesh, ripped from the prey by the front teeth, was most likely gulped down in large chunks.

THE EARLY THERAPSIDS

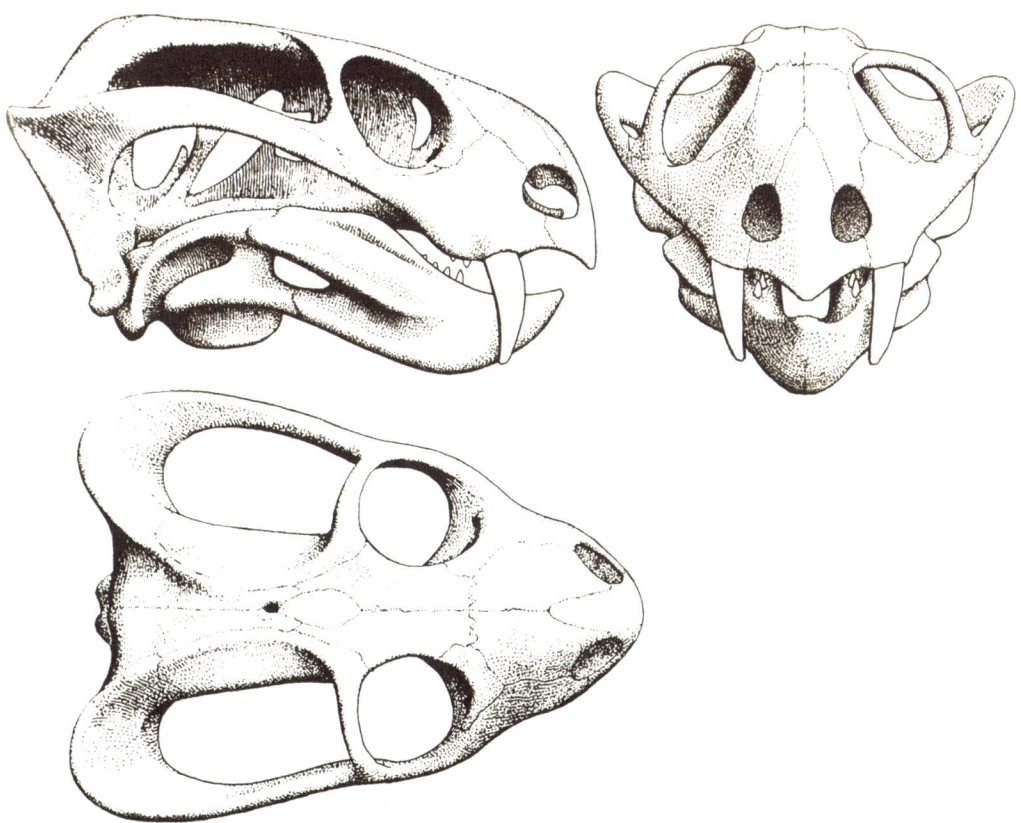

Three views of the Upper Permian dicynodont *Emydops*. This small animal had only a pair of tusks in the upper jaw and few small teeth in the palate and lower jaw. Upper and lower horny, tortoise-like beaks on the jaws were used for slicing and crushing vegetation. The temporal opening behind the eye socket was very large in dicynodonts and housed powerful jaw-closing muscles. The skull is approximately eight centimetres long.

Several advanced therocephalians occurred together with these gorgonopsians. Small, possibly insect-eating forms such as *Scaloposaurus* were present, as well as the specialised Whaitsia where, like the contemporary Gorgonopsia, the rear of the tooth row was greatly reduced. Whaitsids and *Scaloposaurus* were both highly evolved therocephalian groups and important new features seen in the tooth row of scaloposaurids are the tiny cusps on the postcanine teeth. Cusped teeth, of which these were early examples, are important characteristics of mammals, and much of early mammalian classification revolves around the nature of complicated tooth cusp patterns.

Descendants of these scaloposaurids persisted into early Triassic times and a related form, *Bauria,* was a specialised herbivore with flat-crowned crushing teeth. Once considered to be close to mammal ancestry, *Bauria* is, in fact, an advanced member of the therocephalian stock.

A new dicynodont, *Lystrosaurus,* made its first appearance at the very end of the Permian fossil record and was one of the few Permian therapsids to survive into the next chapter of the Karoo fossil record: the Triassic period.

The end of the Permian period – when the earth nearly died

In geological terms, the end of the Permian period 250 million years ago signalled the beginning of the next stage of the earth's history – the Triassic period. However, the fossil record across the world shows that a vast number of species became extinct at this time, both on land and in the oceans. It has been referred to as a point in time when life on earth was nearly extinguished – the Great Dying. Indeed, only a very small percentage of animal species survived this catastrophic time – the **greatest mass extinction event** recorded. In the Karoo, the previously abundant and diverse dicynodonts were reduced to a few species. The Therocephalia disappeared almost completely, with only a few groups surviving into the Triassic, while the Gorgonopsia and the pareiasaurs became totally extinct.

While the end-Permian extinction event was a worldwide one, the record of the Karoo fossil reptiles indicates a series of earlier, relatively minor extinctions which may well have occurred in other parts of the world. For example, the dinocephalians, which were the most significant of the early mammal-like reptiles, disappeared after the fairly short period during which they were the dominant animals. Also, the dicynodonts, which had diversified into a large number of different species, went into a decline before the end of the Permian at a time when evidence suggests that the Karoo Basin was becoming a drier environment. Yet these creatures, with their unusual jaw features apparently making them able to feed on a variety of vegetation types, proved to be adaptable enough to survive in small numbers and species into the early Triassic environments, and to flourish later in the Karoo and other parts of the world.

Lystrosaurus is a fine example of such a survivor. However, little *Diictodon*, so abundant in the Permian fossil records in many parts of the world, disappeared completely – to the extent that if fossil-bearing rock formations are found to contain remains of *Diictodon*, they are almost certain to be of Permian age, and no younger.

It is interesting to note that, while marine sediments of late Permian and early Triassic times around the world provide most of the evidence relating to this extinction event, a small number of extremely important Karoo localities in the eastern Cape and southern Free State have exposures spanning the actual boundary between the latest Permian and the earliest Triassic, providing almost the only terrestrial evidence there is of the effects on land animals of this event, as well as extremely important indications of environmental change captured in the rock formations. These localities are subject to intensive study, and the Karoo fossil and geological record on its own provides us with the most detailed information on the effect and possible causes of the catastrophe that struck the world 250 million years ago.

How was life on earth affected?

Naturally, the cataclysmic end-Permian extinction event raises many questions, the most important being:
- What caused this huge impact on life on earth?
- What caused such a mass extinction of so many groups of animals on such a global scale?
- How were both land- and ocean-living species affected at the same time?
- Is an event such as this likely to happen again in the future?

Dicynodonts of the genus *Diictodon* in the Karoo as it may have appeared during the Upper Permian times about 255 million years ago. In *Diictodon* the tortoise-like beak replaced all the teeth except, in some cases, the pair of tusks in the upper jaw. *Diictodon*, like so many other Karoo animals, did not survive the end of the Permian period.

THE END OF THE PERMIAN PERIOD

We must step away from the Karoo for a moment to get a worldwide picture of extinction patterns in oceans and on land at the time:

- **Marine organisms:** Worldwide, marine invertebrates suffered most heavily, with several groups, including the trilobites, disappearing completely and others, such as the ammonites, reduced to two or three percent of their Permian record.
- **Insects on land:** The Permian period was characterised by a very large diversity of insect species; some of these were the largest that ever existed. However, the end-Permian extinction event was the only one of its kind which had an impact on insects, with several major orders disappearing completely and others greatly reduced.
- **Land plants:** Land plants also suffered severely. *Glossopteris*, a common seed fern in the Karoo and elsewhere, and *Cordaites* (a gymnosperm) went into decline and were replaced by new plants in the succeeding Triassic period.
- **Land animals:** Evidence shows that worldwide more than two-thirds of amphibians and reptiles died at the end of the Permian. A few reptile groups, although very reduced in species, survived briefly into the Triassic before disappearing completely. However, some survivors of the Permian succeeded in adapting to the new environments, and eventually diversified to form new Triassic faunas.

What was the most likely cause of the extinction event?

The earth's record indicates a number of extinction events which have taken place both before and after the end-Permian period. A wide range of possible factors leading to such worldwide extinctions have been proposed, but we will look at only a few of those which could possibly relate to the mass disappearance of so many species at the close of the Permian period:

A meteorite or asteroid strike?

A first possibility that arises is that of an asteroid or very large meteorite striking the earth at the end of the Permian, causing wide-ranging and disastrous effects on living organisms. Evidence for such an impact should be found in existing rock formations: An impact as large as one which could cause such worldwide changes to both plants and animals in oceans and on land should leave traces such as shocked quartz in rocks close to the area of impact. For a while, such shocked quartz samples in Antarctic and Australian rocks were considered as evidence, especially as they are dated as being close to the end-Permian extinction event. However, detailed analyses showed that these quartz samples may have been affected by other geological factors, raising doubt that these were possible indications of an asteroid impact. Again, even if an asteroid had struck in an ocean where crater formations would have disappeared long ago, there would have been evidence in late and post-Permian land rock formations of widely dispersed ejected elements such as iridium. To date, such evidence has not been detected, yet an asteroid impact could lead to major volcanic eruptions and severely affect the environment.

Asteroid strikes have happened in the past: A good example is the giant crater left by a large asteroid in Arizona in the United States, but the largest one known is that which struck what is now South Africa just over two billion years ago. The Vredefort Dome, a geological formation resulting from this vast impact, is named after the Free State town closest to this site.

There is also strong evidence of a very large asteroid impact in what is now the Gulf of Mexico, at the end of the Cretaceous period – about 60 million years ago. This is thought to have affected the world to such an extent that many plants and animals – including the dinosaurs – became extinct.

More about this later.

A very large volcanic eruption?

This possibility seems to be one that would satisfy many questions about the Permian extinction event. At the end of the Permian period, massive eruptions of volcanic lava occurred in northern Pangaea and are today preserved as massive piles of basalt rock formations in Siberia. These basalt eruptions, appearing mainly as huge floods of lava, are one of the largest known volcanic events on earth, covering over two million square kilometres of present-day northern Russia with thick layers of lava. Today the resulting rock formations in this region form impressive mountain ranges. The effects of this event would have been that dust clouds and acid-laced water vapour rose into the atmosphere, disrupting photosynthesis processes and thereby causing food chains to collapse. Ash and other debris would have been flung into the air, while in addition hot lava penetrated thick coal beds – setting them alight and releasing huge amounts of carbon, which settled into water bodies and rendered them toxic. Lava entering shallow seas in the eruption area would have released vast amounts of methane, a greenhouse gas that causes global warming. Indeed, evidence indicates that temperatures at the time increased by six degrees at the equator – and even more in higher latitudes. Seas would have suffered a severe lack of oxygen as well as dangerously high levels of hydrogen sulphide (which might have been the reason for the wide extinction of marine animals). Release of hydrogen sulphide into the atmosphere would have poisoned animals and plants and weakened the ozone layer, exposing life to fatal levels of ultraviolet radiation. A long-term buildup of greenhouse gasses, carbon dioxide and methane may have caused the climatic belts of the world to shift, resulting in the temporary breakdown of the ocean/atmosphere hydrological cycle that controls the earth's rainfall generating system. Such interference with rainfall belts would have been a major factor leading to the disappearance of so many species of land animals and plants.

Widespread changes in the oceans?

One theory is that movements in the earth's crust could have released toxic material into the oceans of the world, which changed the marine environment to such an extent that most sealife came to an end. Such a dramatic change in the oceans would also have affected life on land globally and could have accounted for the extinctions we find among animals that lived on land at that time. But evidence left in the seafloor to support this theory is nearly impossible to find. We know that over millions of years continents have "drifted" relative to each other and that a spreading seafloor in various parts of the earth has been being forced down into subduction zones – a geological "recycling" process.

Any evidence of changes in the seafloor at the end of the Permian period has long since been "recycled" through subduction processes and disappeared completely. But it is interesting to speculate on whether the massive Pangaea supercontinent was slowly starting to break apart at this time. Evidence is that the full-scale break-up began in the early and middle Jurassic period, much later than end-

Permian times, but instability within this huge landmass may well have resulted in changes in the oceans which would have had direct effects on marine and terrestrial life across the globe.

Could such a catastrophic event happen again?

While we know a great deal about the earth and its crust which supports the continents we are familiar with, there is also much that we still do not know. For example, another major volcanic eruption on the scale of what we understand to have taken place in Siberia at the Permian-Triassic boundary could in theory occur again in the future. We are familiar with regular volcanic eruptions along the string of active or semi-active volcanoes along the fault lines where plates of the earth's crust meet and develop pressures between them; these are experienced as sometimes devastating earthquakes and volcanic eruptions – the latter spewing lava and gas from deep within the earth. It would be comforting to think that a new eruption on the scale of that of the Siberian one 250 million years ago is unlikely, but we know that the earth is not a static, frozen-in-time planet, but one which is constantly under pressure from deep below the surface. Our planet is consequently disturbingly unpredictable.

Again, we know that meteors and small asteroids sometimes pass close to earth's orbit – and there have been many instances where they enter the atmosphere and "burn out" before reaching land, but there is a good record of meteorites which have struck land – and which date back to times long past. Many of the smaller ones are now museum specimens. So a strike by a large asteroid cannot be ruled out as a future threat, and an ongoing astronomical survey of nearby areas of our solar system is in place to detect any such a body found to be heading in our direction.

While the theories above can all be possible explanations for the end-Permian extinction event, research into many aspects of the geology and marine environment at the end of the Permian period continues. A final conclusion that will explain all aspects of the extinction of so many land animals and plants, as well as the disappearance of so many marine species, is still awaited.

We can record recent extinctions of animals and plants as nature follows its course, but the major changes in our environment today and increasing pressures on living organisms are largely due to the rapid expansion of the human populations, accompanied by industrial activities that contaminate our environment – affecting even the most remote parts of our planet. Today indications of worldwide climate change are becoming increasingly difficult to ignore – too many instances of cold or warm extremes, too many devastations from fires or drought make us wonder: Are we unwittingly helping the onset of the next extinction event?

The later therapsids

The Permian extinction event was a kind of filter which allowed a few of the therapsids to emerge in the early Triassic. In the Karoo, examples of these include a number of dicynodonts, such as *Lystrosaurus* and the tiny *Myosaurus*. **Lystrosaurus** was equipped with a pair of tusks and the standard dicynodont beak and is thought to have spent much of its time in and around pools and ponds. However, it was clearly also adapted to the new hot and dry environments of the early Triassic. *Lystrosaurus* radiated into several species and fossils of these are found in abundance today at certain Karoo localities. In addition, *Lystrosaurus* became somewhat of an "international" figure during the first stages of the Triassic, with fossil remains found in India, Russia, China, Antarctica, and possibly also Australia.

Together with *Lystrosaurus* lived several early members of the mammal-like **Cynodontia**. These animals, very likely descendants of the Permian Therocephalia, show several advances over other therapsids and are regarded as the forerunners of the first true mammals. Important features which indicate an approach to mammal status include a direct contact between the dentary bone of the lower jaw and the squamosal bone at the rear of the skull – such as in humans. Others are indications of body fur or whiskers on the snout. These, together with the strong likelihood that these small

Animals besides *Lystrosaurus* which lived in Lower Triassic Karoo times were *Chasmatosaurus* (top), a 1,5-metre-long early archosaurian reptile; *Capitosaurus* (centre), a large amphibian; and the cynodont *Thrinaxodon* (bottom), a 25-centimetre-long therapsid.

animals were nocturnal and active at night, all point to evidence of endothermy – the ability to maintain a constant body temperature, even in cold environments. Endothermy is one of the fundamental characteristic of true mammals.

The small cynodont **Thrinaxodon** shows many of the characteristic of the cynodonts. Especially striking are the postcanine teeth, each of which carries several well-developed cusps. However, upper and lower tooth rows did not meet during chewing and biting activity, and the cusps are not worn into facets as seen in mammals. Another advance over more primitive therapsids seen in *Thrinaxodon* is the development of a bony secondary palate in the roof of the mouth. This structure, universally present in mammals, serves to shift the internal opening of the respiratory passage to the back of the mouth. As a result, the animal is able to chew food in the front of the mouth and breathe at the same time. A high metabolic rate, such as required by warm-blooded mammals, requires uninterrupted respiration, and it is clear that *Thrinaxodon* and other cynodonts were approaching the mammalian grade.

Other parts of the *Thrinaxodon* skull show equally significant refinements. The sides of the skull and braincase are further developed than in earlier forms, and the larger brain is therefore better protected. In the lower jaw the tooth-bearing dentary bone is, in mammalian

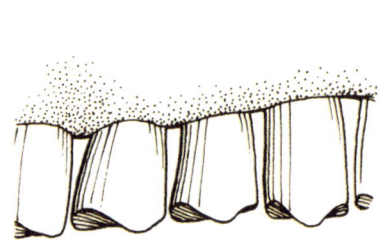 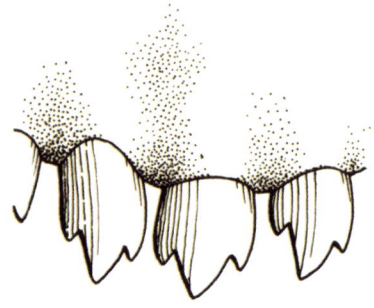

LEFT: Teeth of the advanced therocephalian *Bauria*, adapted for crushing vegetation in the mouth. **RIGHT:** Teeth of the primitive cynodont *Thrinaxodon* showing a number of simple cusps.

THE LATER THERAPSIDS

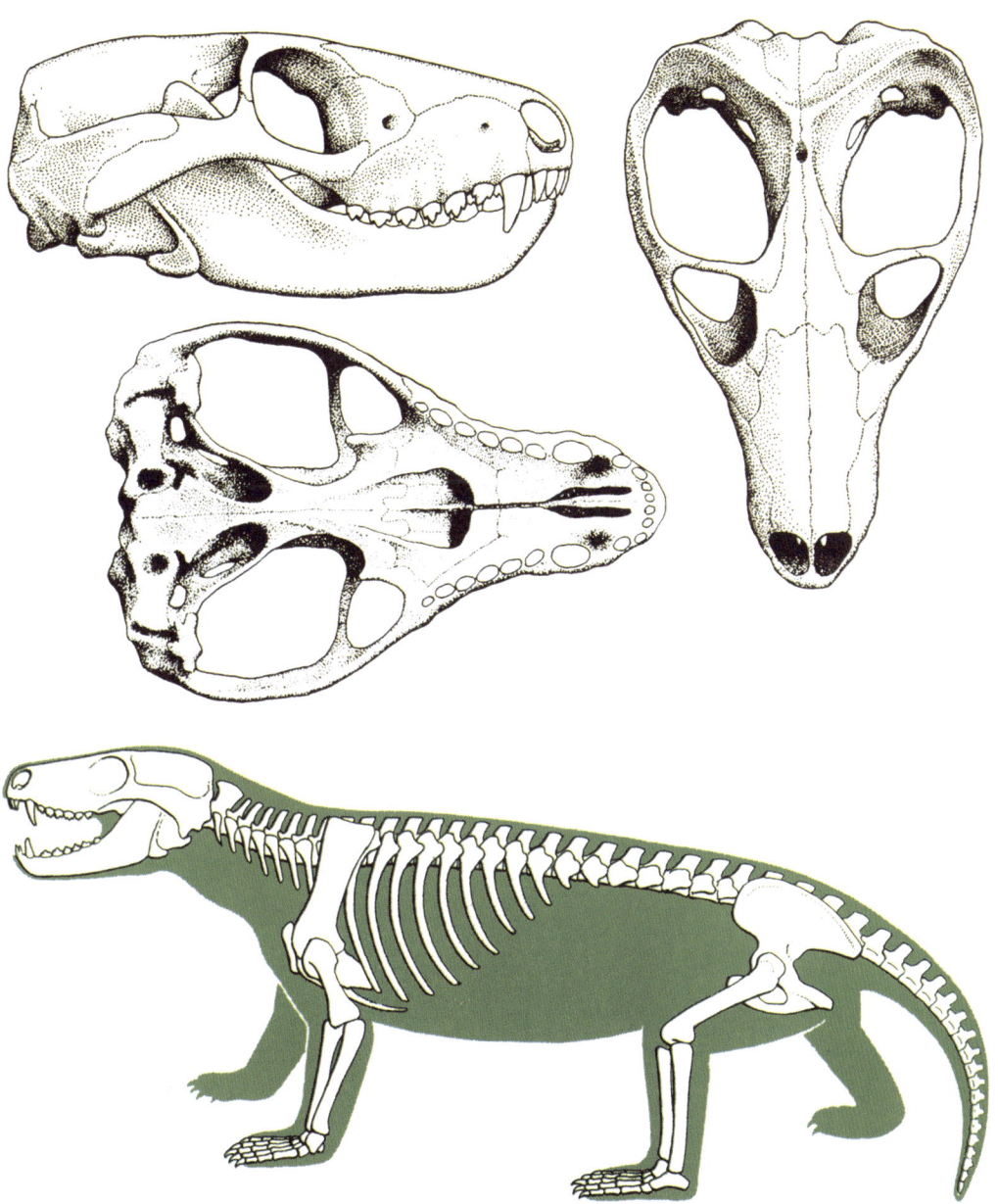

TOP: Three views of the skull of *Thrinaxodon*. In the right-side view (top left) the tooth row, consisting of incisors, canines and cusped molar-like teeth, can be seen, as well as the tooth-bearing dentary in the lower jaw. In the ventral underside of the skull (bottom left), a sheet of bone forms a mammal-like secondary palate between the tooth rows. **BOTTOM:** Skeleton and body outline of *Thrinaxodon,* an early Triassic cynodont with a number of advanced mammal-like features. Body length was about 0,5 metres.

fashion, considerably enlarged while the other lower jaw bones are correspondingly reduced in size.

The primitive *Thrinaxodon* is well removed from the immediate ancestry of mammals, but later cynodonts, present in the warmer and drier environments of the later Triassic, show some of the changes that brought the group close to the mammal boundary. Fossils of *Cynognathus,* an advanced cynodont, were first identified in the Karoo's Triassic-age rocks but have since also been found in South America and Antarctica.

In the late Triassic *Lystrosaurus* was totally absent and dicynodonts were represented by the much larger *Kannemeyeria*. But the range of animals approaching mammal status was varied and plentiful. *Cynognathus* was a powerful flesh-eating cynodont, but plant-eating types such as *Diademodon* and *Trirachodon* were also present. In *Trirachodon* transversely elongated upper and lower teeth met during the chewing process and food was actively broken down in the mouth before being swallowed.

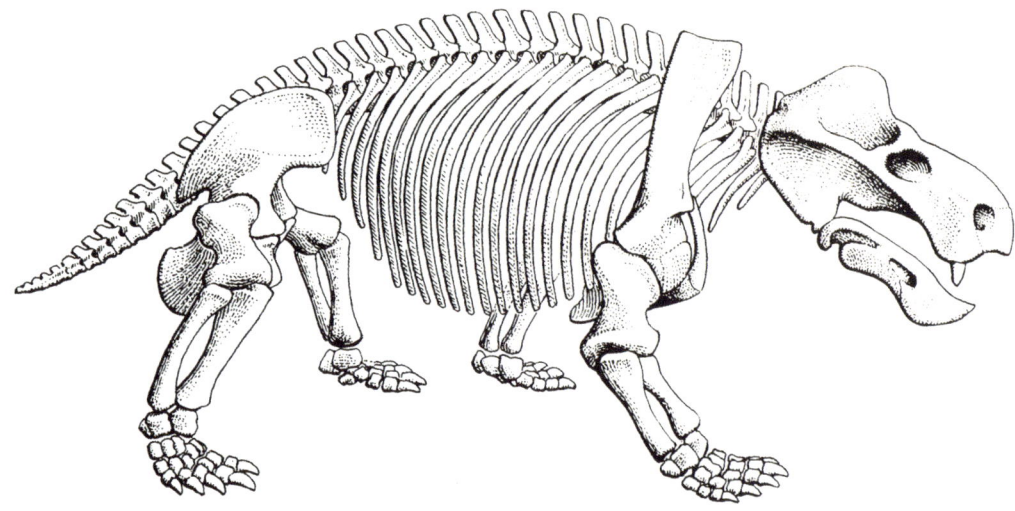

Skeleton of *Kannemeyeria*, a two-metre-long dicynodont of the Triassic *Cynognathus* zone. This was one of the last Karoo dicynodonts, but animals related to *Kannemeyeria* persisted until the end of the Triassic in other parts of the world.

THE LATER THERAPSIDS

TOP: The 12-centimetre-long skull of *Tritylodon*, an advanced therapsid from the Upper Triassic period of the Karoo. With its rodent-like teeth *Tritylodon* was once regarded as one of the first true mammals.
BOTTOM: The skeleton of *Megazostrodon*, regarded by many scientists as one of the earliest mammals known. With a body length of around 13 centimetres, *Megazostrodon* is from the Upper Triassic series of the Karoo and was probably a nocturnal insect-eating animal.

Another highly specialised group, known as the tritheledontids or ictidosaurs, were small- to medium-sized animals where the lower jaw dentary bone was actually connected to the skull and effectively formed the entire lower jaw. By this characteristic and evidence that whiskers may have been present on the snout, the group could be classified as mammals. However, other features suggest that they were approaching the mammalian grade independently of the true cynodont-mammal line.

As yet, no specific cynodont can be confidently pointed to as being a direct ancestor to the first mammal. However, among the many forms that show trends – some in parallel fashion – towards the **mammal boundary**, a line can be discerned leading from an early *Thrinaxodon*-like animal through a succession of more advanced forms to culminate in the first true mammals in late Triassic times. *Diarthrognathus* is an especially interesting advanced form. Here the lower jaw and skull meet in such a way that two bones of the lower jaw meet two bones of the upper jaw of the skull. One small evolutionary step would result in two of these bones becoming part of the three tiny bones found in the mammalian middle ear, resulting in a fully mammalian jaw joint between the dentary bone of the lower jaw and the squamosal bone of the skull. The early Jurassic *Pachygenelus*, known from tiny skull fragments found in the late Karoo rocks, appears to be very close indeed to claim mammalhood status, while in the late Triassic/early Jurassic rocks in the central Karoo – below the Drakensberg mountain range – the equally tiny skulls and partial skeletons of *Megazostrodon* have recently been accepted as having reached the mammal grade. So there can be little question that by the end of the Karoo period a new class of animal was making an appearance and standing at the threshold of the Age of Mammals.

The final stages of therapsid evolution took place in a Karoo environment very different from that of earlier times. The climate had become increasingly hot and dry, and the Karoo rock layers of that time, named the Elliot Formation, reflect this, while the succeeding sandstone layers of the Clarens Formation – the last of the fossil-bearing Karoo geological succession – were formed in semidesert conditions where windblown sand covered much of the region. Finally, the fossil record in the Karoo Basin ended abruptly with a series of **major volcanic outbursts**; streams of lava flowed over the landscape and built up to a huge thickness capping the succession of Karoo rocks. Today these volcanic rock formations, known as the Drakensberg basalts, form the towering Drakensberg Mountains in the central and eastern parts of South Africa.

In the late Triassic and early Jurassic Karoo, therapsids and their mammalian descendants were small animals which together formed an insignificant part of the total fauna. From their overwhelmingly dominant position in the early times of the *Tapinocephalus* assemblage zone, they were now, in turn, dominated by newcomers to the Karoo – the dinosaurs and their relatives.

The archosaurs – a new wave of reptiles

Therapsids were by no means the only inhabitants of the Karoo Basin. From early times they were accompanied by a number of creatures which were representative of the true reptiles. One group, of which *Youngina* is an example, is known from the Upper Permian and appears to be connected with the ancestry of lizards and snakes, while *Mesosuchus*, a reptile from the early Triassic, is an early member of the Rynchosauria – one of the earliest branches of an important group known as the **Archosauria**. The Archosauria in turn lead us

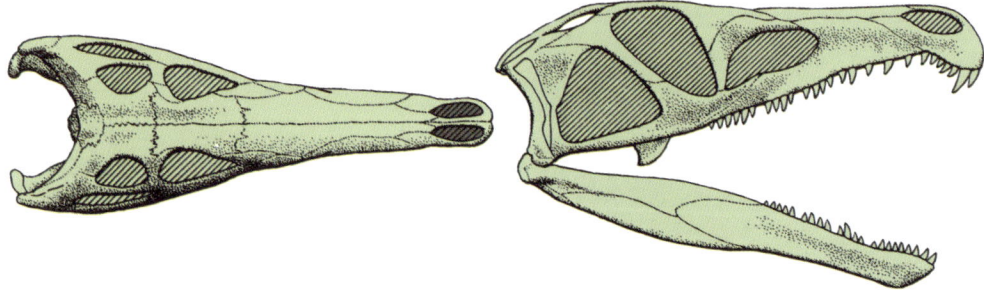

TOP: Skull of the primitive archosaur *Chasmatosaurus*. The skull is very different from that of any therapsid and has two openings behind and one in front of the eye socket. The teeth are simple and pointed and not divided into different tooth types as in many therapsids and true mammals. The skull was approximately 40 centimetres long.

OPPOSITE TOP: The primitive archosaur *Euparkeria,* from the Lower Triassic *Cynognathus* zone of the Karoo. This reptile, about 65 centimetres long, was related to the ancestors of dinosaurs, crocodiles and birds. *Euparkeria* probably raised itself onto its hind-legs when running. **OPPOSITE BOTTOM:** Skeleton of the six-metre-long *Massospondylus,* an early South African dinosaur. *Massospondylus,* of which many fossils have been found in the early Jurassic period of the Karoo, may have been able to rear itself up onto its hind-legs, but probably also used all four legs when walking.

THE ARCHOSAURS

to another contribution which the Karoo fossil record has made to science – the origins of crocodiles, dinosaurs and birds.

Recent years have seen a great deal of research and discussion on what have previously been generally referred to as "dinosaurs" and their relatives. Remember, palaeontologists have mostly incomplete specimens to work on, so comparing one set of bones with others is difficult. But new discoveries of fossils across the world – some of them nearly complete – have thrown fresh light on the relationships between these most interesting (and well-known!) animals, and the picture which has now emerged is very different from what was generally accepted a few decades ago.

First of all, there is now wide agreement that the Archosaurs include two major groups – the Saurischia and the Ornithischia.

The first group, the **Saurischia**, led to the origin of pterosaurs, dinosaurs such as the Theropoda and Sauropoda, and the ancestors of birds. Theropods include a number of carnivorous dinosaurs such as the coelurosaurs and the gigantic *Tyrannosaurus*. Sauropods include massive plant-eating dinosaurs such as *Brachiosaurus*, *Apatosaurus* and *Brontosaurus*. The second group, the **Orthithischia**, include the large predatory Rauisuchidae, which appear to be confined to the Triassic period, herbivorous dinosaurs such as *Triceratops* and the stegosaurs, as well as early crocodiles. These two groups, Saurischia and Ornithischia, therefore together include what are generally known as "dinosaurs".

In South Africa, the Triassic and early Jurassic rocks of the Karoo have revealed a number of representatives of these dinosaurs. *Plateosaurus* is a sauropod known from the Triassic of the Karoo, as is *Massospondylus* (one of the first dinosaurs to be discovered), while the small *Heterodontosaurus* is an early representative of the ornithischian line of later dinosaurs. More about these dinosaurs later.

The herbivorous prosauropod dinosaur *Massospondylus* (front) and *Melanorosaurus* (back). The 12-metre-long *Melanorosaurus* was one of the larger types of dinosaur found in the Karoo's late Triassic rocks.

THE ARCHOSAURS

In addition, fossils of early **crocodiles** such as *Orthosuchus*, *Protosuchus* and *Sphenosuchus* have been found in the latest Upper Triassic and early Jurassic rocks of the Karoo. These crocodiles were archosaurs, such as the dinosaurs discussed above, but were only distantly related. These were largely terrestrial creatures (unlike their living descendants), some with long limbs – possibly for rapid movement. *Notochampsa* is the largest of these primitive crocodilians, with a skull of ten centimetres long. *Orthosuchus*, one of the best known of these early crocodilians, probably also inhabited streams and pools of the Upper Triassic and early Jurassic environment. Although generally small, with a skull length of not more than ten centimetres, animals such as *Erythrochampsa* and *Orthosuchus* possessed most of the features of living crocodiles, sometimes only in rudimentary form. For example, the extensive secondary palate which is seen in living crocodiles and functions in the same way as in mammals is only partially developed in a Triassic crocodile ancestor such as *Orthosuchus*. The armoured crocodile *Notochampsa* is found in early Jurassic rocks and is the last Karoo representative of this group.

Early Karoo archosaurs such as *Proterosuchus*, *Prolacerta* and *Euparkeria* were neither crocodile nor dinosaur, but possessed many of the characteristics that distinguish the group as a whole. The skull, in comparison with that of therapsids, was loosely constructed. Where therapsids had a single opening for muscle attachments on the side of the skull behind the eye socket, archosaurs had two, and an additional opening is found between the eye socket and nostril on the side of the skull. The lower jaw consisted of several bones and the teeth were simple and sharp-pointed, much as in modern crocodiles, and the body was frequently protected by rows of bony plates.

Proterosuchus lived alongside *Lystrosaurus*, but had many of the habits of modern crocodiles. Clearly a predaceous animal, it very likely spent much of its time in pools or on the banks of streams on the lookout for small or young individuals of *Lystrosaurus* or the amphibians common at the time. *Euparkeria*, smaller than *Proterosuchus*, was a lightly built, partly bipedal animal. Although it lived later than *Proterosuchus*, it retained more primitive features and its skeleton had many of the characteristics of both dinosaurs and crocodiles.

While creatures such as *Proterosuchus* and *Euparkeria* formed an important part of the contemporary fauna, it was not until the dinosaurs appeared that archosaurs became the dominant group in the Karoo. Early dinosaurs such as the sauropods *Massospondylus*, *Euskelosaurus* and *Melanorosaurus* were common in later Triassic times while others such as the ornithischians *Heterodontosaurus* and *Lesothosaurus* survived into the early Jurassic period.

Lesothosaurus and *Heterodontosaurus* are among the earliest ornithischians known. In these bipedal and plant-eating animals, the teeth in the rear of the upper and lower jaws lie in packed rows and vegetation was broken up in the mouth by crushing and slicing movements between the upper and lower tooth rows. In some ornithischians the front teeth were replaced by a horny beak, somewhat similar to that found in dicynodont therapsids.

Dinosaurs differed in several important respects from living reptiles such as lizards or crocodiles. Recent research has reinforced earlier suggestions that at least some dinosaurs were not "cold-blooded" and could in fact maintain a reasonably constant body temperature and a high metabolic rate. Dinosaurs appear to have achieved this in a manner altogether different from that of mammals, and it seems that their metabolic mechanism was generally much better suited for the warm late Triassic conditions than was that of the early mammals. Older concepts of dinosaurs being slow-moving and sluggish creatures have today been replaced by suggestions that these huge monsters were, in fact, active and highly mobile and, in some cases, fleet of foot. As shown in a later section, these physiological advances were to stand dinosaurs and their relatives in good stead in succeeding periods.

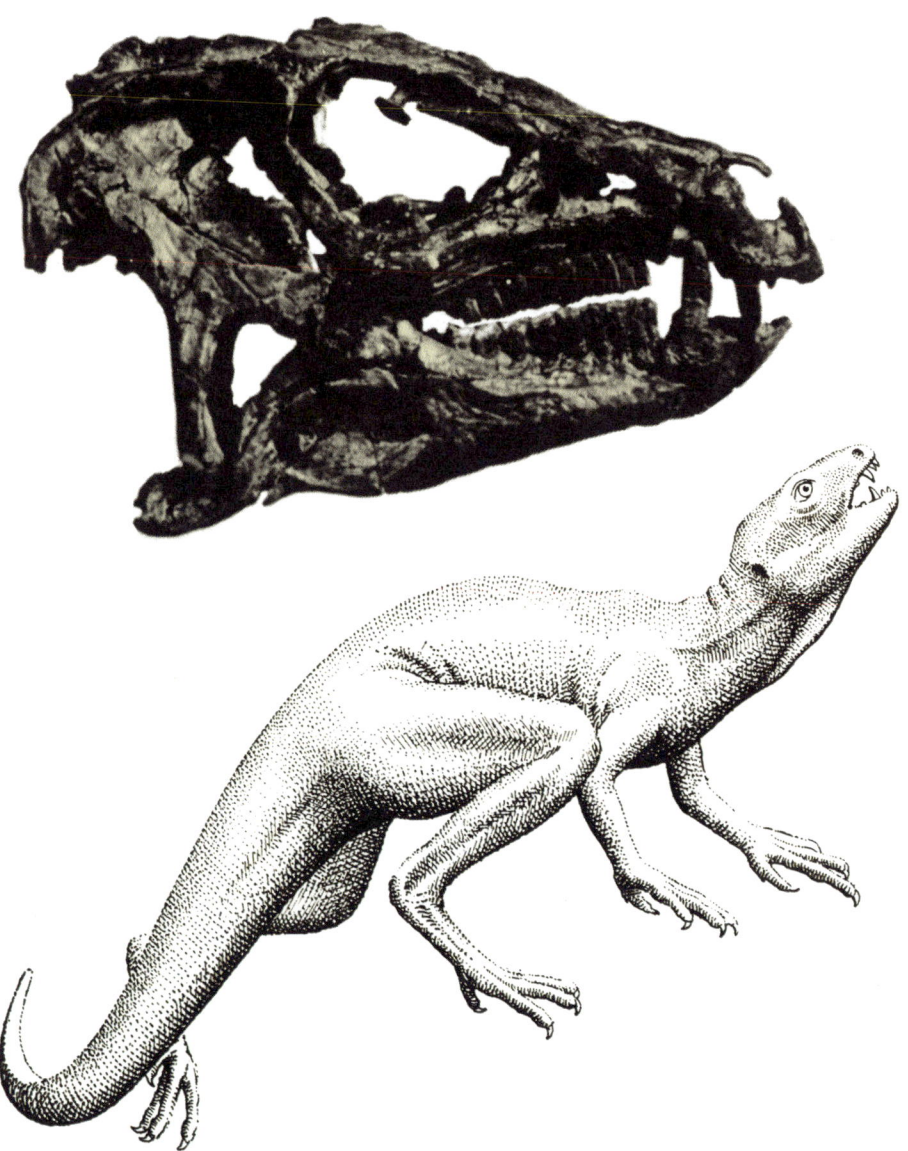

The skull and lower jaw of the dinosaur *Heterodontosaurus* (top) and the reconstructed animal as it may have appeared in life (below). *Heterodontosaurus,* with its specialised teeth adapted for crushing vegetation, is one of the earliest known representatives of an important dinosaur group, the Ornithischia. The total length of the animal was about one metre.

OPPOSITE: The herbivorous prosauropod dinosaur *Massospondylus* (front) and *Melanorosaurus* (back). The 12-metre-long *Melanorosaurus* was one of the larger types of dinosaur of the Karoo.

THE ARCHOSAURS

The **Karoo dinosaurs** did not achieve the massive proportions or bizarre appearances of later dinosaur groups, but the herbivorous *Melanorosaurus*, which had a body length of up to twelve metres, would have been an impressive animal. *Massospondylus*, which seldom reached more than a relatively modest six metres in length, was a partly bipedal plant-eater and is known from several nearly complete skeletons. In the region around Clarens in the Free State, below the Drakensberg Mountains, *Massospondylus* eggs, some with

the fossilised embryos intact within the shells, were discovered some years ago and were recognised as the earliest dinosaur eggs known. More recently, a massive plant-eating dinosaur, *Ledumahadi mafube*, was discovered in the same area; this dinosaur would have weighed twelve tons and stood at four metres high at the hips.

The last Karoo dinosaurs were by no means the end of dinosaur development in Africa. In fact, an increasingly wide distribution of later Jurassic and Cretaceous dinosaurs is now known from sites in South Africa as well as other parts of the continent. Dinosaur remains have been found in Algeria, Niger, Zimbabwe, Egypt and Tanzania. These dinosaurs provide an important spectrum of dinosaur variety over a very wide area and provide evidence of the relationships between these animals with those in other parts of the world. In South Africa, a number of recent discoveries in the eastern Cape have revealed several new localities where dinosaur remains have been found. Near the town of Sterkspruit a remarkable dinosaur bone bed – a kind of prehistoric graveyard – has revealed a number of new dinosaurs, while a number of sauropod dinosaurs of Cretaceous age have also been discovered in an area close to Port Elizabeth.

The fossil crocodile *Orthosuchus* (top) and the reconstructed animal (below). Although the *Orthosuchus* reached a length of 70 centimetres and lived nearly 200 million years ago, it already had many of the characteristics of today's living crocodiles.

The Karoo fossil animals and the ancient supercontinent Gondwana

We now know that at the time when the story of South Africa's Permian and Triassic reptiles was unfolding, all the present-day southern continents formed part of Gondwana, which was itself part of the supercontinent Pangaea. **Gondwana** achieved the status of geological independence when it parted from Pangaea at around 170 million years ago. The rest of Pangaea became the nucleus of the present-day northern continents – Eurasia and North America. Later, Gondwana became divided into a few smaller continents and landmasses. Today these "fragments" of the once-great Gondwana are familiar to us as Africa, South America, Madagascar, Australia, Antarctica and India.

Naturally, the concept of a large single Gondwana landmass during the Permian and Triassic which later fragmented to become a number of smaller, separate continents explains much about the distribution of fossils of the extinct animals found in the Karoo in what are today distant parts of the world. For instance, if fossils of the same species are found in rocks of continents now widely separated from each other, it can be argued that at the time when these animals were alive the continents were close enough together to provide a single area of distribution. In fact, long before continental drift, seafloor spreading, and the concept of Gondwana became part of our modern understanding of the earth's geology, several Karoo fossils were used to show that the arrangement of the earth's continents must once have been different to what we see today.

The small reptile *Mesosaurus*, mentioned earlier, was discovered long ago in rocks of Lower Permian age in both southern Africa and

THE KAROO FOSSIL ANIMALS AND GONDWANA

Brazil and, since it would not have been possible for the delicate *Mesosaurus* to have made its way across a great South Atlantic ocean between Africa and South America, it seemed reasonable to believe that Africa and South America once lay close together. Interestingly, a close relative of *Mesosaurus* has recently also been found in Madagascar, which at the time also lay close to the east coast of present-day South Africa.

Another Karoo reptile which illustrates the results of continental drift is the therapsid *Lystrosaurus*. Fossils of *Lystrosaurus* were known from Lower Triassic rocks in South Africa, India and Sinkiang in China well before a dramatic discovery by geologists working in Antarctica showed that *Lystrosaurus* lived on that continent as well, 250 million years ago. In Australia, a skull fragment has been identified as being that of a species of *Lystrosaurus*. Not to be left out of this picture, fossils of the cynodont *Cynognathus* have now also been found in South America and Antarctica.

Evidence shows that India broke away from Gondwana and "drifted" north until it reached Asia. The **Himalayas**, the greatest mountain range on earth, are a grand monument to this ancient collision and a sober reminder of the huge forces involved in continental drift. Antarctica, on the other hand, was forced southwards into high latitudes and became covered in thick layers of ice. The fossils of *Lystrosaurus, Cynognathus* and a recently discovered skeleton of *Thrinaxodon* found in rocks rising out of this glacial wilderness are evidence of a time when Antarctica enjoyed a more hospitable climate than it does today.

After the discoveries in Antarctica, a more recent find of a *Lystrosaurus* specimen in Russia showed that this dicynodont was one of the most cosmopolitan of land animals in the early Triassic, and it is possible that further prospecting in South America and other continents will uncover even more fossils of this ancient world-traveller.

Other Karoo fossils – *Diictodon* is an example – have been iden-

THE KAROO FOSSIL ANIMALS AND GONDWANA

Skull of *Lystrosaurus* (top), a dicynodont common in the Lower Triassic of the Karoo, and the animal (below) that was widespread over parts of Gondwana and the northern continents, showing that there was once a time when these continents lay close to Africa.

tified in rocks of similar age to those of the Karoo on other continents and South Africa's Karoo fossils, therefore, should not be considered in isolation from other parts of the world. At the time when these creatures were the most advanced land animals on earth there were no Atlantic or Indian oceans, and it made little difference to an animal whether it lived in what is now Bengal in India, the Transantarctic mountain region in Antarctica, Sinkiang in China or Harrismith in South Africa's Free State. But with the break-up of Gondwana, living plants and animals – and the fossils in the rock formations under them – effectively became passengers on a number of breakaway landmasses to new homes on our planet.

The record of South Africa's Karoo fossils is a fascinating and intriguing one, but it becomes all the more remarkable when viewed in the light of the geological phenomenon of continental drift.

The destiny of the early dinosaurs and mammals of the Karoo

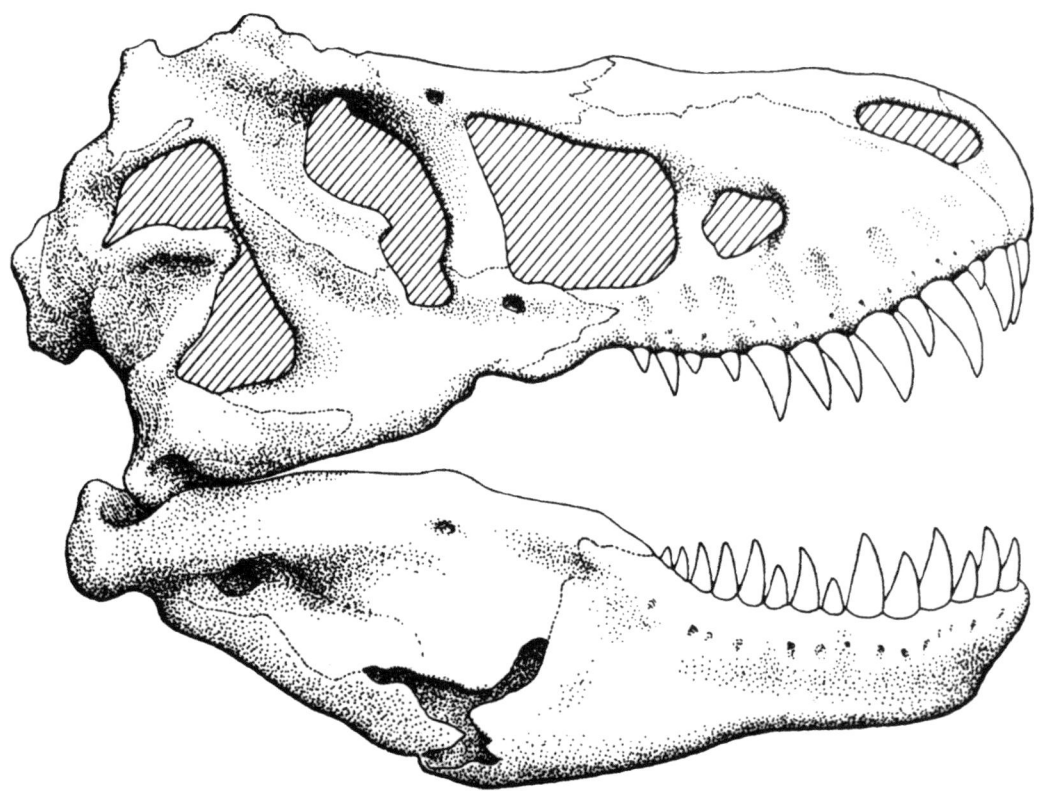

The 1,3-metre-long skull of the giant dinosaur *Tyrannosaurus*, perhaps the most awesome flesh-eating creature which ever existed. *Tyrannosaurus* is known from the Upper Cretaceous rocks of North America.

By the end of the Karoo times in the early Jurassic, therapsids and archosaurs had achieved a wide distribution in areas outside southern Africa. So when volcanic activity 190 million years ago turned the Karoo into an inhospitable wasteland, it is possible to follow the subsequent evolutionary history of the two groups from fossils in other continents.

THE DESTINY OF THE EARLY ANIMALS IN THE KAROO

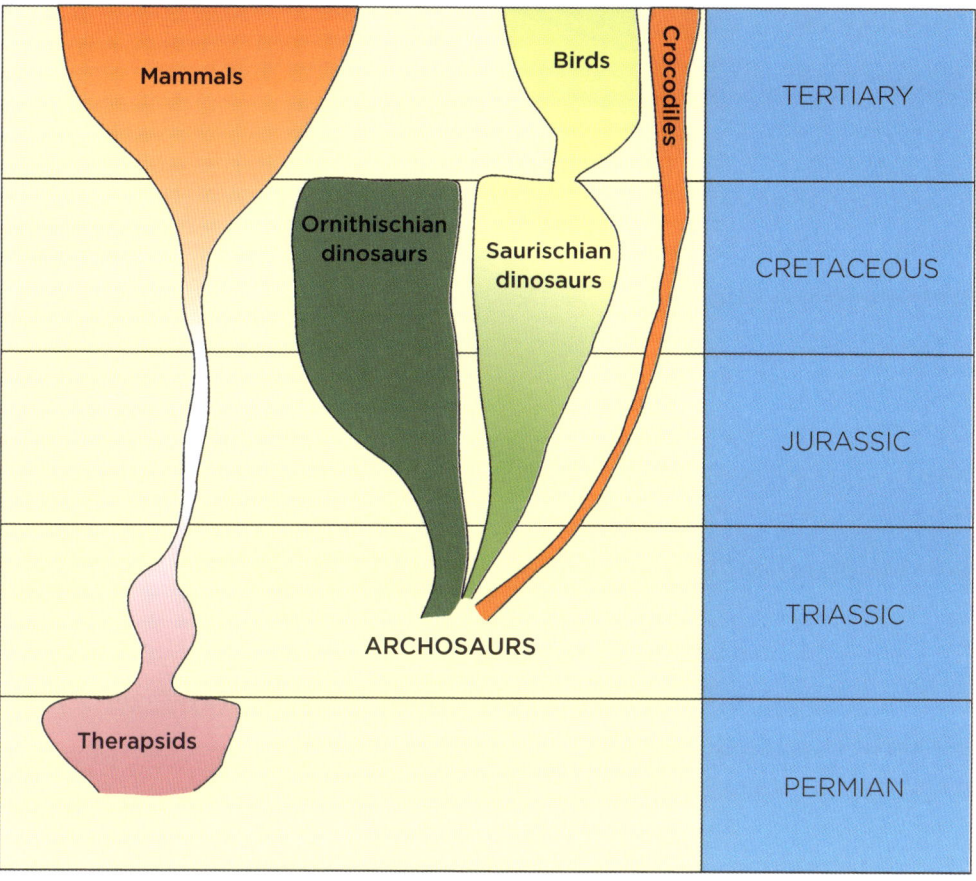

This chart illustrates how, during the Permian, Triassic and early Jurassic periods, fossils of the Karoo can show when the first mammals arose from therapsids, how the earliest archosaurs gave rise to the first dinosaurs and crocodiles, and how, much later, the first birds arose from Saurischian dinosaurs.

While the Therapsida did not survive beyond the early Jurassic, their descendants, the **early mammals**, underwent a minor radiation into a number of families. Almost always small, these animals are rare in the fossil record and therefore poorly known, and it seems that for many millions of years mammals remained a minor group in a world dominated by other animals. However, in the following Jurassic and Cretaceous periods, together representing a time span of over 130 million years, the radiation of dinosaurs resulted in overwhelming numbers of medium-sized to very large animals. Some, such as the nine-metre-long *Tyrannosaurus*, were among the most formidable predators known, while the plant-eating *Diplodocus* reached a length of 27 metres. *Diplodocus* and its relatives such as *Brachiosaurus* were among the largest four-legged animals known. *Brachiosaurus*, for instance, reached a body length of some 24 metres and had a body mass approaching 50 tons.

But the reign of the dinosaurs ended abruptly at the close of the Cretaceous period, 65 million years ago. **Dinosaur extinction**, as well as the extinction of a great many other species, is perhaps one of the best-known events of palaeontology. One theory holds that large-scale volcanic activity caused worldwide changes in environments – much like one of the theories for the cause of the end-Permian extinction event. However, a now widely accepted theory is that a massive asteroid impact resulted in sudden change of climates and environments around the world, affecting all living animals and plants to varying degrees.

A geological feature supporting this latter theory is a 150-kilometre-wide impact crater found under the Yucatán Peninsula in the Gulf of Mexico. Intensive studies have shown that this massive crater was formed by the impact of a huge **asteroid** – between 11 and 15 kilometres in diameter. The crater, now largely covered by subsequent rock formations, is estimated to have been 20 kilometres deep. Such an impact would have caused huge tsunamis and earthquakes as well as disastrous effects on the earth's atmosphere; huge ocean waves would have raced over the seas and land. In North America, at least two localities have been found where jumbled fossils of fishes, trees and reptiles – including dinosaurs – lie mingled together, an indication of the enormous effect the impact had on the earth.

Finally, the date determined for this impact event is precisely the time that the dinosaurs and many other creatures disappeared from the fossil record.

This gigantic asteroid strike and the subsequent effects on the

84 THE DESTINY OF THE EARLY ANIMALS IN THE KAROO

THE DESTINY OF THE EARLY ANIMALS IN THE KAROO

earth's atmosphere and climates are most likely the reason for the extinction of dinosaurs and many other creatures.

At the same time, the changes that had proved so fatal to the mighty dinosaurs were very likely the same ones that pushed the early mammals to the front of the evolutionary stage. The dawning of the Tertiary period 65 million years ago ushered in the great **Age of Mammals**, of which we are a part today. From the descendants of the Jurassic and Cretaceous mammals sprang the huge diversity which we are familiar with, such as bats, whales, antelopes, moles and our own humankind.

But are the dinosaurs really totally extinct? Earlier, we saw birds included within the theropod dinosaur group. In fact, there has for many years been evidence for a close relationship between dinosaurs and birds – the fossil Jurassic-age bird-like *Archaeopteryx* discovered in Europe in the nineteenth century led to much discussion about its possible relationship with dinosaurs and the first birds. Current opinions are that *Archaeopteryx* was not an ancestor of birds, but nevertheless had a close relationship to both dinosaurs and the first true birds.

In fact, new evidence from the fossil record of **birds** has led to the realisation that these animals, which are "warm-blooded" and, as we well know, extremely active, are evolutionary descendants of a group of flesh-eating theropod dinosaurs. Recent finds in several continents of fossils of feathered "dinosaurs" with bird-like skeletons have shown that, in a quirk of nature, dinosaurs are to this day still represented in the form of birds in our modern animal kingdom. In

PREVIOUS PAGES: The dinosaurs *Tyrannosaurus* (left) and *Diplodocus* (right) known from North American fossils. Mighty dinosaurs such as these lived well after their Karoo forerunners had died out, and for many millions of years they held sway as the dominant land animals of the earth. *Note*: Although shown together in this illustration, the Upper Cretaceous *Tyrannosaurus* lived sometime after *Diplodocus*, which is from the Upper Jurassic age.

fact, dinosaurs as a group are now being divided into two subgroups: "non-avian dinosaurs", which includes ornithischian and saurischian dinosaurs, and "avian dinosaurs", which includes both fossil and modern-day birds. This view is becoming increasingly supported as fresh fossil finds are made across the world and it is now evident that, while their dinosaur relatives succumbed to extinction at the end of the Cretaceous period, "early birds" passed through the Cretaceous/Tertiary boundary relatively unaffected and ready to multiply into the many thousands of species we know today and which give colour and song to our gardens and forests.

Just as interesting is the fact that **crocodiles** – classified as archosaurs – also survived the end-Cretaceous calamity. So today's birds – so full of energy – and the relatively slow-moving but highly dangerous crocodiles lurking in rivers and mud banks, are now the only representatives of the mighty dinosaurs which dominated the earth for so many million years.

The evolutionary pendulum has swung many times in the past and will doubtless continue to do so in the future, each movement ushering in a time for new species to rise and dominate others. The fossil animals of the ancient Karoo swamps and marshes give a unique and invaluable insight into the emergence of the land vertebrates we know today, and the fate of the many that lived before them.

Collecting and preserving Karoo fossils

The fossil-bearing strata of the Karoo Sequence, making up the Beaufort and Stormberg groups, covers an extensive part of the present-day South African landscape and fossil occurrences are theoretically possible in any part of the area.

To be meaningful, **fossil collecting** requires the experience and technical training of the professional palaeontologist, and although the layman can be of great assistance to the scientist in locating fossils in the field, it is essential that any amateur should work in close collaboration with a recognised scientific institution. By making use of what is known of Karoo geology, field parties of scientists can predict with a fair degree of certainty the type of fossil and its relative

Recovering two partial skeletons of *Aulacephalodon*, a large dicynodont which lived in the late Permian period. The fossils were discovered near Fraserburg in the Western Cape and took ten days of hard work to remove. (Photographs: Roger Smith)

COLLECTING AND PRESERVING KAROO FOSSILS

Prof. Roger Smith with the overturned partial skeleton of a *Pareiasaurus* encased in a plaster jacket and ready for transport to the preparation laboratory for careful removal of all rocks covering the ancient bones. (Photograph: Roger Smith)

BOTTOM: A team removing a skeleton of *Lystrosaurus* near the town of Bethulie in the Free State. Rock has been carefully dug away around the fossil and the plaster jacket covers the exposed bones. The next step is to carefully loosen the jacket and skeleton from the rock underneath and turn over and secure the whole slab – fossil, rock and plaster jacket – for safe transportation. (Photograph: Roger Smith)

age in any particular region. Nevertheless, many areas in the Karoo are as yet incompletely explored and the search for new localities, as well as new specimens, is an important part of the palaeontologist's work.

Strata of different ages of the Karoo are exposed in several classic localities, some of which have been known since the nineteenth century. The earliest and most primitive fossils occur in the region south of Beaufort West, and can be found in the districts of Laingsburg, Prince Albert, Sutherland and Beaufort West itself. Later forms, such as *Endothiodon* and *Cistecephalus,* can be found in the Beaufort West, Murraysburg, Graaff-Reinet and Fort Beaufort areas, while *Lystrosaurus* and contemporary forms are common in the late Permian to early Triassic rock exposures around Middelburg (Cape), Bethulie, Harrismith and Bergville. Classic localities of later Triassic fossils, such as *Cynognathus,* lie around Aliwal North and Burghersdorp, while Late Triassic and the earliest Jurassic forms such

as the early dinosaurs and the rare remains of immediate ancestors of true mammals can be found in the uppermost beds of the Karoo, surrounding the Drakensberg mountain range, in the Fouriesburg, Hershel and Matatiele districts.

These areas, which are only a few of known **fossil-rich areas**, are important for collecting purposes because of the abundance of fresh rock exposures. When a fossil is exposed to the weathering influences of wind, water and temperature fluctuations, it – like the surrounding shale and sandstone – begins to split or crumble, and the best localities are usually those where soft shale layers are exposed as fresh, smoothly rounded slopes with a minimum cover of soil and vegetation. In such localities, fossils are recognised as lumps or nodules on the shale slopes or in the debris along dry watercourses leading from the shale slopes. The typical Karoo "koppie" is often the only vertical relief in an otherwise flat landscape, and shale exposures along its sides, if free of vegetation or thick layers of weathered rocks and soil, are often the source of well-preserved fossils.

Once a fossil has been identified as such, the task of **extraction** begins – not always an easy exercise because in most cases the fossil is extremely delicate and sometimes ready to disintegrate if not carefully handled. Using a protective, fast-drying glue to coat all visible pieces of bone, the fossil is carefully exposed by chipping away surrounding rock with hammer and small chisels until the full extent of the specimen is uncovered. Often a protective jacket, made of reinforced plaster of Paris, is necessary for the final extractions and removal of the find. Care is taken to ensure that every part of the specimen is collected, including the smallest rib fragment or toe bone. At the same time, all available locality data is recorded, in-

Nieu-Bethesda, not far from Graaff-Reinet, in the heart of the Karoo. The landscape is dominated by exposures of Upper Permian rock sediments, rich in fossils. The Kitching Fossil Exploration Centre is located here.

cluding the date of the discovery, the exact position of the fossil and its relationship to adjacent sandstone or shale layers, the geographical coordinates of the site, and any other associated fossilised plant or animal remains. Without this information, a specimen – no matter how rare or complete – loses much of its scientific value.

Before it can be properly studied and compared with other specimens, the fossil must undergo a sometimes lengthy and painstaking process of **preparation**, during which it is freed from surrounding rock, or matrix, as this is called. Most fossil preparation requires the use of sophisticated apparatus, including dental drill and probes, and is done under a binocular microscope. In certain cases, the rock matrix may be removed by immersing the fossil in dilute acid, and considerable extra detail – particularly in the skull – may be

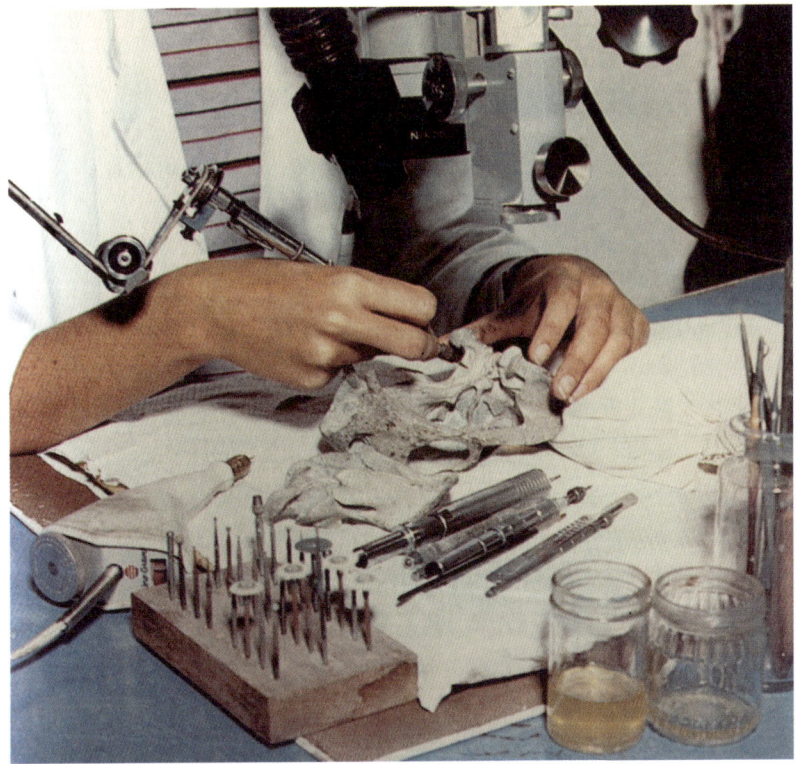

In the laboratory where microscopes and fine tools are used. Great care is taken not to scratch or break even the most delicate fossil bones buried for more than 200 million years.

obtained in this way. No two fossils are exactly alike and the method of preparation of any particular specimen is a matter to be carefully decided upon and may combine a number of different techniques. In some cases a specimen – especially if small and delicate – may be X-rayed to provide detailed information on fine structures which are beyond the scope of conventional preparation.

The preparation laboratory is a vitally important section of any palaeontological institution, since it is on the skill of the preparators that the final result – the fully prepared and restored fossil specimen – depends.

Collecting, preparing and restoring fossils are therefore integral parts of palaeontological research and are not tasks to be undertaken without experience and supervision. It cannot be sufficiently stressed that fossils, such as those of the prehistoric Karoo, are all-too-rare traces of past life and should be regarded not as curiosities but as scientifically important items of evidence essential to our understanding of the origin and evolutionary history of life on earth.

The **National Heritage Resources Act of 1999** can issue permits to professional scientists to search for and collect fossils. If by any chance you stumble upon what appears to be a fossil embedded in rock, your best option is to contact your nearest museum and advise the appropriate staff of your find. You can bear in mind that some of the most important fossil finds known were first discovered not by professional scientists, but by people with keen eyes who did the right thing and reported the fossil find to allow proper excavation to be undertaken. In fact, many of the most important known fossils have been named after the people who found them and drew them to the attention of palaeontologists.

Where to see fossils in southern Africa

If you are interested in fossils and past life on earth in general, there are many opportunities for finding out more about the subject. Some of these may be quite close to you:

Western Cape:
- The Iziko South African Museum in Cape Town has excellent exhibitions of Karoo fossils as well as African dinosaurs.
- The West Coast Fossil Park near Langebaan has ongoing excavations of late Tertiary fossils – mammals, birds, whales, three-toed horses and more – as well as a fine display in the museum building.
- At the Karoo National Park, on the N1 just south of Beaufort West, a "fossil trail" featuring Karoo fossils from the surrounding region is open to the public.

Free State:
- The National Museum in Bloemfontein, with fine displays of Karoo-age and other fossils.
- Florisbad, some way out of Bloemfontein, is where the "Florisbad Man" skull was discovered in 1932. Florisbad is one of South Africa's Middle Stone Age fossil localities.

Eastern Cape:
- The Graaff-Reinet Museum has a special exhibition of Karoo fossils on display. This collection of fossils is from the Graaff-Reinet district, and nearly all the specimens were located by the late Lex Bremner.

- At the nearby Nieu-Bethesda is another new exhibition of fossils from the area, celebrating the work of South Africa's best-known fossil collector, the late James Kitching.
- The Albany Museum in Grahamstown has a fine collection of fossils from the region on display in this, one of the oldest museums in South Africa.
- The East London Museum is home to the famous Coelacanth, a true "living fossil" of hundreds of millions of years earlier, and a surviving member of a primitive group of fishes of which fossils have been found in the Karoo fossil record.
- The Port Elizabeth Museum's Bayworld has fossils and reconstructions of dinosaurs on display.

KwaZulu-Natal:
- The Natal Museum in Pietermaritzburg has a fossil collection on display.
- The Durban Natural History Museum also has fossils on display.

Gauteng:
- Witwatersrand University houses the Origins Centre with fine exhibitions of fossil ancestors of modern humankind. Wits is the leading institution for palaeontological research in South Africa and houses extensive collections of fossils. The university also maintains the Kitching Fossil Exploration Centre in Nieu-Bethesda that displays fossils from the surrounding Karoo.
- Visit the Cradle of Humankind at Maropeng about 50 kilometres northwest of Johannesburg where many hominid fossils have been discovered.

Namibia:
- Pay a visit to the Mesosaurus Fossil Camp near Keetmanshoop where many specimens of *Mesosaurus* have been found and can be viewed. Remember that South America, where other *Mesosaurus* specimens occur, is just across the South Atlantic to the west …

SUGGESTED FURTHER READING

Besides books such as these listed below, the internet provides up-to-date information on new fossil discoveries around the world, as well as the latest published findings and theories on the origins and relationships between extinct animals.

Alvarez, L.W., Alvarez, W., Asaro, F., Michel, H.V. (1980). *Extraterrestrial cause for the Cretaceous-Tertiary extinction.* Science: 208: 1095–1108.

Alvarez, Walter (1997). *T. Rex and the Crater of Doom.* Princeton University Press.

Benton, M.J., Twitched, R.J. (2003). *How to kill (almost) all life: the end-Permian extinction event.* Trends in Ecology and Evolution 18: 358–365.

Chinsamy-Turan, A. (2008). *Famous Dinosaurs of Africa.* Struik.

Chinsamy-Turan, A. (Ed.) (2011). *Forerunners of mammals.* Indiana University Press.

Chinsamy-Turan, A. (2014). *Fossils for Africa.* Cambridge University Press.

Kammerer, C.F., Angielczyk, K.D., Fröbisch, J. (Ed.) (2014). *Early evolutionary history of the Synapsida.* Springer.

Kemp, T.S. (2005). *The origin and evolution of mammals.* Oxford University Press.

Kidder, D.L., Worseley (2004). *Causes and consequences of extreme Permo-Triassic warming to globally equable climate in relation to Permo-Triassic extinction and recovery.* Palaeogeography, Palaeoclimatology, Palaeoecology 203: 207–237.

SUGGESTED FURTHER READING

King, G.M. (1990). *The Dicynodonts: a study in palaeobiology.* Chapman and Hall.

Norman, N., Whitfield, G. (2006). *Geological Journeys: a traveller's guide to South Africa's rocks and landforms.* Struik.

Retallack, G.J., Smith, R.M.H., Ward, P.D. (2003). *Vertebrate extinction across the Permo-Triassic boundary in the Karoo Basin, South Africa.* GSA Bulletin 115: 1133–1152.

Rubidge, B., McCarthy, T. (2006). *The story of earth and life, a southern African perspective.* Struik.

GLOSSARY

Archosauria – a large and important branch of reptiles, which appeared during early Triassic times. Archosaurs are represented today by crocodiles, and birds are thought to be highly modified descendants of an early group of archosaurs. Extinct archosaurs include dinosaurs and flying reptiles.

Asteroid – a small body lying in the solar system between the orbits of Mars and Jupiter. Asteroids are larger than meteors and can reach sizes of a kilometre and much more. Asteroids have struck the earth in the distant past – the most recent impact event occurred in northern Russia in 1908 when a small asteroid broke up just before reaching ground in the Tunguska area.

Bipedal – animals that walk or run on their back legs, leaving their front legs to collect food or defend themselves.

Cynodontia – a group of advanced therapsids, including both plant- and flesh-eating types, regarded as being ancestral to the first mammals. Cynodonts flourished during Triassic times.

Dentary – the tooth-bearing bone on the lower jaw. In reptiles it is only one of several jaw bones, but in mammals the dentary forms the entire lower jaw on each side. The dentary becomes progressively larger during the evolution of mammal-like reptiles to mammals.

Dicynodontia – a specialised branch of therapsids which lasted through nearly the entire Karoo period. Dicynodonts were plant-eating animals and had tortoise-like upper and lower horny beaks.

Dinocephalia – an early, relatively short-lived branch of therapsids, characterised by large-sized and, in some cases, very thick skull bones.

GLOSSARY

Dinosaurs – extinct archosaurian reptiles which lived from Upper Triassic times to the end of the Cretaceous period. Mostly large or very large animals, dinosaurs included flesh- and plant-eating types. The two main groups of dinosaurs are the Saurischia and Ornithischia.

Evolution – the slow process of natural biological change resulting in the appearance of new types of animals or plants from earlier ones.

Extinct organism – a plant or animal known from fossilised remains which has no living descendants.

Fossilisation – the process by which the hard parts of animals or plants become preserved in rock as fossils. Rocks which contain fossils were formed from the mud, clay or sand which covered the plants or animals.

Gorgonopsia – a group of carnivorous therapsids, which inhabited the Karoo swamps until the end of the Permian period, about 225 million years ago.

Ornithiscia – one of the chief groups of dinosaurs, which included *Heterodontosaurus* of the Karoo's Red Beds. Ornithischian dinosaurs included only plant-eating types.

Palaeontologist – a scientist who studies the fossilised remains of extinct plants and animals.

Primitive – retaining original characteristics of earlier, ancestral groups. Therefore, primitive features in the skeleton can link an animal to an ancestor which lived perhaps many millions of years earlier.

Saurischia – one of the two chief groups of dinosaurs, which included the early Karoo prosauropods *Massospondylus* and *Melanorosaurs* as well as the later *Tyrannosaurus* and *Diplodocus*.

Sedimentary rocks – rocks, such as sandstone and shale, that formed out of hardened clay, mud or sand, usually in a watery environment. Fossils occur only in sedimentary rocks.

GLOSSARY

Squamosal – a bone in the skull lying behind the eye socket and above the connection between the lower and upper jaws.

Temporal opening – an opening between the bones of the temporal region of the skull, behind the eye socket, to allow space for the main jaw-closing muscles. Therapsids had a single temporal opening, whereas dinosaurs and crocodiles had two. Primitive reptiles such as the pareiasaur *Bradysaurus* retained the original, closed temporal region of ancestral reptiles.

Terrestrial – adapted for life on land.

Therapsida – an important group of fossil reptiles which bridged the gap between true reptiles and the first mammals. Therapsids combined many of the characteristics of reptiles with those of mammals and became extinct at the end of the Triassic period, 200 million years ago.

Therocephalia – a group of therapsids, mainly carnivorous but including some late, specialised plant-eating types. Therocephalians probably gave rise to the more advanced Cynodontia before becoming extinct in Triassic times.

Zone – in this book a zone refers to a layer of sedimentary rock containing the same types of fossil throughout. Based on reptile fossils, the Karoo has been divided into a number of zones, lying one on top of the other.

ACKNOWLEDGEMENTS

I am indebted to comments and suggestions from Dr Hamish Robertson, Prof. Roger Smith, Prof. Bruce Rubidge and Dr Jonah Choiniere, which have been most helpful and have added much value to the content of this book. I wish to thank them for making this project possible. Ms Rooksana Omar, CEO of Iziko Museums of South Africa, encouraged me to write a new version of the old *Karoo Reptiles of the South African Karoo,* and I thank her for her support. Thank you to the Protea Book House editorial team, and Zaituna Skosan, Marietjie du Toit and Frans Pietersen for making this venture possible. Finally, I would be sadly amiss in not mentioning the untiring assistance of my editor. Danél was always available for advice, was unashamedly critical of some of my suggestions, and was a pleasure to work with. Thank you, Danél!

M.A. CLUVER

DR MICHAEL CLUVER grew up in Stellenbosch. He obtained his M.Sc degree in Zoology at the University of Stellenbosch. After his studies he took up a position at the South African Museum where he worked under Dr L.D. Boonstra, a leading palaeontologist with a wide knowledge of the Karoo fossils. He concentrated his research on the dicynodont *Lystrosaurus*, one of the few Karoo therapsids to survive the end-Permian extinction event, and received his Ph.D degree based on this work.

Focusing mainly on dicynodonts, he continued with his research before being appointed Assistant Director and later Director of the South African Museum. Over the years, he has done research at the Natural History Museum in London, the American Museum in New York and the Smithsonian in Washington. He retired in 2007, but continues to work part time at the new Iziko Museums of South Africa.